Magnetic Nonprofit

Attract and Retain Donors, Volunteers, and Staff

Jeremy Reis

Magnetic Nonprofit

© 2019 Jeremy Reis

ISBN-13 978-0-9760043-2-5

Nonprofit Donor Press

http://magneticnonprofit.com

Edited by Esther Martinez.

Early praise for *Magnetic Nonprofit*

Jeremy Reis is a gifted young leader in fundraising who is very missional, creative and committed to building donor relationships in a way that lasts. He clearly understands the core essentials necessary to help you build a healthy nonprofit that compounds its growth and can make an impact for generations. I highly endorse *Magnet Nonprofit*!

— E. Dale Berkey, President, BBS & Associates

When I was President of Food for the Hungry in the early 2010s, I knew Jeremy as a person and colleague of integrity, passion, and deep understanding of the fundraising and non-profit marketing world. After reading his newest book on the *Magnetic Nonprofit*, I now know Jeremy as a first-rate author and practitioner who shares game-changing truths, concepts and advice for any and everyone who wants to do a better job being "sticky" when it comes to attracting and keeping passionate and committed donors and other partners. I highly recommend this book!

— David Evans, President, LifeNet International

In *Magnetic Nonprofit*, Jeremy Reis reveals the essentials of connecting and capturing the hearts of those who will care the most about your mission. (*And this isn't just about donors!*) Based on research and personal experience, he identifies the barriers to engagement and the practical ways you can overcome each of them. In these pages, you will discover how to accomplish the God-sized vision for your nonprofit by inspiring passion, building trust, and rallying the commitment of many!

— Tami Heim, President, CEO, Christian Leadership Alliance

Very few marketers and fundraisers know that the secret to acquiring and retaining more customers and donors does not happen through promotion, but rather through attraction. In his seminal work, the *Magnetic Nonprofit*, Jeremy Reis distills the six attributes to making your organization more attractive and then takes you on a journey inside a $140 million nonprofit that proves that the system actually works.

— Timothy M. Kachuriak, Chief Innovation and Optimization Officer, Next After

In my 45 years of nonprofit development work, this is one of the best books I've found on attracting donors—and accomplishing the even harder mission of retaining donors. This book is filled with common sense advice many nonprofits overlook. You'll find stories and inspiring content that creates a perfect recipe that will be invaluable to nonprofit organizations that want to advance and fund their mission to make the world a better place. Read this book today! You will not only be inspired as a nonprofit leader, but you'll also be equipped to inspire and motivate fellow staff, board members, donors, volunteers, and ultimately, the people you serve.

— Mike King, President/CEO, Youthfront

Magnetic Nonprofit is a delightful guide full of important insights for those working in donor acquisition and fundraising. Jeremy Reis' expertise and research take us on an eye-opening journey into the world of attracting and retaining donors, volunteers and staff. How to be successful? His six T's are compelling to get started. Thanks, Jeremy, for sharing your findings with us.

— Cécil Van Maelsaeke, Head of Marketing, Communication and Fundraising, Tearfund Belgium

Magnetic Nonprofit is so beautifully simple and straightforward. If you follow the principles and expert guidance that Jeremy puts forward, you'll build deeper donor relationships and raise more money.

— Andrew Olsen, Partner, NEWPORT ONE

The *Magnetic Nonprofit* is a must-read for anyone in the nonprofit fundraising industry. Jeremy Reis has captured so many practical insights from years of hands on experience. If you are committed to donor growth and culture change, I highly recommend you read this book!

— Kristin Smith, VP of Integrated Marketing and Development, Christian Aid Mission

Magnetic Nonprofit is an Insider's Guide to growing a healthy nonprofit through consistent and effective communications. Jeremy Reis pulls back the curtain and provides a simple framework for nonprofit practitioners seeking predictable increase in donor giving, volunteer engagement and staff retention. If you're looking for engaging case studies, compelling research and pragmatic instruction, *Magnetic Nonprofit* is for you.

> — Marc Stein, Co-Founder of The Global Center for
> Nonprofit Excellence

To my wife Jennica and children, Emily, Evie, Julia, Ellie, Elijah, Josiah, Isaiah, Selah

Contents

Foreword

Regardless of religious persuasion, political affiliation, or cultural identity, there is one beautiful attribute of the human spirit that I have firsthand and consistently witnessed all over the world: people want to help other people that are hurting. If we see someone hungry, we want to feed them. If we see an entire community drinking water from a swamp, we want to provide clean and safe water to them. If we see a child sick or injured, we want to help them find medical care and heal to full strength.

There are many different approaches and theories on the most effective ways to alleviate human suffering, but that does not change the innate desire that we all share to help others. That desire is likely why you picked up this book in the first place!

Person by person, the loving action of serving someone else is a deep part of the human experience. And you especially know this to be true if you have ever been on the receiving end of someone's care and compassion. There is one aspect to this equation that is troubling - there is only so much impact that each of us can have individually. Whether we like it or not, there is simply no way for you or I to serve many hundreds, thousands, or millions of people on our own. We need resources, we need structure, we need professional skills, and we need a team of like-hearted people to serve on mission with us.

It is for this very reason that nonprofit organizations exist. There are too many more people in need than we can possibly help on our own. As one person, I am physically unable to provide food for hungry children living in the inner city of Chicago, or clean water to thousands of families in Ethiopia, or urgent medical care needed for those caught in the middle of a violent civil war in Syria.

As one person joining together with many others – donors, professional staff, volunteers, and community stakeholders – we can make real and lasting change possible at a level of scale that far exceeds what would be possible on our own effort. That is the power of the nonprofit organization when it is operating effectively and efficiently in the execution of its mission. And that is what the Magnetic Nonprofit will help you do.

For too long, nonprofit organizations have not utilized best practices. We have been powered by the best of intentions and a genuine desire to be of service. No longer are good intentions and desires sufficient. There is simply far too much at stake in our world today for nonprofit organizations and the staff that lead them to be satisfied with sub-par quality in the name of good intentions. We can do better, and when we do better, we serve better. This is the whole reason we got involved in this line of work in the first place!

You, the colleagues in our sector, and I must strive toward becoming skilled professionals who thoughtfully balance a deep passion for a cause with technical training and craftsmanship that multiplies the impact of our efforts. We need to learn from research and apply best practices. We need to work together to share resources and reduce redundancy. The good news is that the blueprint for all of these strategies is at the core of the Magnetic Nonprofit.

In the pages that follow, Jeremy generously shares what I'm going to call a 'new baseline.' If each of our nonprofit organizations adopted this 'new baseline' of practice, we would dramatically increase the satisfaction of donors, decrease the turnover of our staff, and better engage the volunteers who serve under our guidance. These best practices will also demonstrably improve relationships with key community stakeholders who will begin to take the quality of our nonprofit work seriously and will reciprocate with investments that accelerate the accomplishment of our shared goals. Magnetic nonprofits serve more people and serve more effectively.

Regardless of the size of your organization or the duration that it has been in existence, my hope is that you will take a few hours over a few weeks and work through these pages with your team to establish the 'new baseline' of best practices that Jeremy has outlined for all of us. If your organization is new and small, go through the book with your Board of Directors. If it is large and well established, find a key influencer on the management team and make sure that they read the book!

In so doing, you will flatten the learning curve and save time and money that you would otherwise have invested in practices that simply do not work. I only wish that this resource would have been available to me 20 years ago when I started serving with nonprofit organizations as a volunteer (with Food for the Hungry, interestingly enough). Even today, operating at the highest level of an international nonprofit organization, I read through this book and grieved the mistakes that I made that could have been avoided had this resource been available earlier.

There is much at stake. Your organization exists to fill a void and provide a service that is much needed. You are a person that wants to help hurting people. And when you are able to draw near the right staff, donors, stakeholders, and volunteers, you will provide the services faster and better than you ever could have thought possible. That is what being a Magnetic Nonprofit is all about.

Justin Narducci
President and Chief Executive Officer
Lifewater International

Introduction

I am passionate about seeing the generosity of others increase.

Some in the nonprofit fundraising industry see total annual giving as one big pie. Each nonprofit takes their small slice of the pie, and if one nonprofit grows, another shrinks. Unfortunately, the numbers could support this line of thinking. In 2018, there was no donor growth. In fact, the industry lost 4.5% of its donors, putting donor growth in the red.

However, I refuse to accept it has to be this way.

The practice of nonprofit fundraising must change, and for that to happen, organizations must change.

When I joined Food for the Hungry (FH) in 2012, we faced several challenges. As we began addressing these challenges, we found it wasn't just one thing that needed to change. We didn't have *just* a fundraising problem. Or *just* a hiring problem. Or *just* a cash flow problem. Or *just* a communication problem between departments. We faced all of these problems, and more.

But, we were committed to change what we could. As we began to transform the organization, we saw a culture shift inside Food for the Hungry. We also saw changes in our donor base. In the past four years, we've seen dramatic results in various fundraising areas because of the work we did over the past seven years. Here's a look at our numbers from the last four years compared to the industry averages, according to the *Fundraising Effectiveness Project* surveys:

	2015	2016	2017	2018
Industry Growth in Revenue	5.3%	3.0%	2.2%	1.6%
FH Private Income Growth	14%	32%	22%	18%
Industry Growth in Donors	2.0%	0.6%	0.75%	-4.5%
FH Donor Growth	4.9%	25.9%	10.4%	6.5%
Industry Renewal Rate	46%	45%	45.5%	45.5%
FH General Donor Renewal Rate*	72%	72%	73%	74%

* Does not include Child Sponsors which has a much higher renewal rate

We've been able to consistently beat industry averages because we didn't address just one problematic area, but we worked to improve multiple facets of the organization.

At the time, I didn't have the "Magnetic Nonprofit" framework to understand what we did. Now, I look back and realize the changes we made resulted in Food for the Hungry improving some of the six Ts: Transparency, Thankful, Tenured, Timely, Testimony, Tribe. Or what I like to call, magnetic attributes.

We didn't get all of them right at first. But, after I developed these magnetic attributes, I began implementing changes in other areas of private fundraising, such as thankfulness. Even this small change had a positive impact on our results. Now, two years after developing the core Magnetic Nonprofit concepts, I've experienced the nonprofit-changing benefits of addressing each of the six attributes.

I have a clear vision for the power and transformation these concepts could have for your nonprofit. It's not going to be easy, but nothing worth doing ever comes easy. Moreover, trust me when I tell you — it's worth it.

It's worth it when you see donors increase their generosity. It's worth it when you have happier staff who accomplish more. It's worth it when you see people jump at the chance to help when you know how limited their time is. It's worth it when *you* are changed because of it.

There isn't just one big pie of generosity with a limited number of slices available. It's an ocean of generosity, and as the tide rises, all ships rise with it. Join me in changing your donors, volunteers, and staff to be more attracted to your nonprofit, and develop an organization that attracts new supporters while strengthening the connection with the ones you have. Join me in transforming your organization into a Magnetic Nonprofit.

The Magnetic Nonprofit

Only 19% of first-time donors give a second gift. This statistic shows us we have a significant problem in the nonprofit industry.

Can you imagine if a major corporation only had 1 in 5 customers return for additional purchases? If a retail store chain lost over 80% of its new customers? If a restaurant only had 19% of customers come back a second time? None of them would stay in business.

No one would accept that number. And we shouldn't either.

Though there are countless reasons why that first-time donor doesn't make a second gift, we need to discover what the most common reasons are and eliminate them. We need to figure out, as an industry, how to retain first-time donors and build a strong relationship with them. We need to increase that percentage so that when we acquire a new donor relationship, we keep it for life.

DONOR RETENTION

Why is it important to retain donors?

Donor acquisition costs are high. The initial cost it takes to find and acquire a new donor is high. For most nonprofits, it can take 18-24 months to recoup the amount of money spent to attract the new donor. Most acquisition campaigns cost 2-3 times the initial donation amount. For example, if we receive an initial donation of $35, it could have cost between $70 and $105 to acquire that donor. We would need multiple donations to break even on that donor.

Potential for increased giving. The *Fundraising Effectiveness Project* study showed that for returning donors with gifts of $100 or less, nonprofits retained 53% of their donors, while for gifts of $250 or more, nonprofits retain 76%. As your donor's relationship matures with your nonprofit, s/he is likely to give more.

Lifetime value of the donor encourages acquisition. For most nonprofits, the lifetime value of the donor is what makes the high acquisition cost reasonable. If, for example, your lifetime value per donor is $500, spending $100 to acquire the donor makes sense.

Happy donors give you access to their friends and family. When you have a donor who is passionate about your organization and cause, you increase the likelihood that s/he will share your fundraising campaigns with his/her tribe, or even start a peer-to-peer fundraising campaign of their own to raise money for you.

Why is the retention rate of new donors so low?

Donors don't feel appreciated. If a donor doesn't feel appreciated after making a gift, she is less likely to give again to the same organization.

Donors didn't understand what impact their donation made. A nonprofit should clearly communicate to the donor what they did with the donation and the impact it had on beneficiaries. Clearly communicating impact increases the chance for a second gift.

Donors gave to support a friend or family member. In peer-to-peer fundraising campaigns, the donor may be giving the gift because of a friend, and not because of the nonprofit or the cause. For example, if someone is running a 5K to raise money for a breast cancer research charity because she has breast cancer, her neighbor may donate because she is a friend. However, this neighbor may not care about the charity itself.

The nonprofit stops communicating. Sometimes, a nonprofit doesn't communicate enough or at all to get the second gift. If a nonprofit is scared to overwhelm new donors, they may swing so far into not communicating that they lose the chance at receiving a second gift.

Though there are numerous reasons why donors stop giving, some nonprofits beat the trends. As a nonprofit fundraiser, this is a crucial problem you must solve.

Which characteristics attract donors, staff, and volunteers to a nonprofit (and keep them)?

In 2016, I began researching to identify why certain nonprofits grow and succeed in their mission, while others are stuck and are barely surviving financially. As the Senior Director of Marketing at Food for the Hungry, this question was immensely significant to my role and the success of our marketing department. I asked myself the following questions: How could we retain more of our donors so we aren't losing so many of them after the first gift? As a $140 million organization, how can we grow to $250 million? $500 million? $1 billion? How can we feasibly and financially help tens of millions of more people and lift hundreds of communities out of extreme poverty? To accomplish these seemingly impossible goals and answer these questions, I explored why some nonprofits beat the trends and why others struggle to find resources.

It can't merely be attributed to the founder's passion, as I've known dozens of nonprofit founders who are deeply committed to their cause.

It's not simply how hard the staff works, as I've seen some of the most creative and hard-working people in nonprofits struggle to meet their vision despite their efforts.

"WHY SHOULD I GIVE TO YOU?"

I knew the answer would be both quantitative and qualitative. It would consist of cold, hard facts and data, but also include stories, the feelings of supporters and staff, and traits that couldn't be explained with just raw data. I started the research for this book with a simple study, based on NextAfter's research study *"Why should I give to you?"*[1]

I asked a simple question using a pseudonym, Jessica, to 167 different charities via email and Facebook Messenger:

My husband and I are looking to donate to a nonprofit like yours. Why should we donate to your organization versus another organization, or not at all? Thanks!

My theory was that organizations that can communicate their brand promise succinctly and persuasively have a higher chance of attracting donors, employees, and volunteers. What I discovered was amazing!

Irrespective of size in terms of revenue, nonprofit organizations in my study did a poor job of responding to this question. In fact, 65 of the 167 organizations didn't respond at all! Many of the organizations that did respond didn't adequately answer the study's question and couldn't tell me why I should support their organization versus a different

---

[1] http://www.nextafter.com/vp

one. As a representative of a nonprofit, you need to (and should) succinctly tell me a support case for your organization. If you can't, you won't be able to attract donors at sufficient numbers to provide long-term support for your cause.

Thirty-seven organizations did respond but didn't answer my question directly. Here are a few example responses (the organization was anonymized):

Dear Jessica,

Thank you for your inquiry. Organization name supports the efforts of local churches in addition to a number of other support avenues for vulnerable people in our world. I hope you take a look at our giving opportunities as illustrated on our website.

Please know we see this as the start of the conversation and hope if you still have questions you will contact us again.

Blessings,

Organization Name

Our original inquiry is begging for a response that sets the organization apart. In this first sample response, the organization gave me a one-liner and then told me to visit their website. Considering I contacted them from their website, it should be evident that I wasn't finding the information to answer my question. Here's another example of an organization that sent me back to the website:

Ms. Andrews,

These are the varied ways in which your donations will be used.

http://www.organization.org/wildlife-conservation

http://www.organization.org/habitat-protection

http://www.organization.org/community

http://www.organization.org/economic

If you have any questions, comments or concerns, we can be reached in the info listed in our signature.

Thanks.

In both cases, neither organization signs the email from a live person but instead uses the organization name in the first email as its signature, and no signature at all in the second example. Contrast these two emails with one of the excellent responses received (this is a religious organization):

Hello, Jessica!

What a fabulous question, "Why should we donate to your organization versus another organization or not at all?"

In order to have sent this inquiry, you must have spent some time on our website. The first answer I would give is to spend some time on the Why India page. This has more information than you are looking for in this email.

So why am I a donor to Organization Name? I will start there. My husband and I attended a fundraising banquet back in 1996, long before I became an employee of Organization Name. We started giving because we were moved in our hearts for the unreached people in India, not the lost in India, the unreached in India. They have literally never even heard the name of Jesus and they have never been given the opportunity to respond. Rom 10:14 "How, then, can they call on the one they have not believed in? And how can they believe in the one of whom they have not heard? And how can they hear without someone preaching to them?"

We gave for many years until our priorities had to focus more on where our kids were at in school and in our local church.

In 2014, I felt called to the position of Regional Associate at Organization Name. I had just graduated from college at the age of 44 and the job market completely changed for me. I had so many more opportunities for employment than I did just two years prior when I had no college degree.

My situation is repeated countless times in India only more so. My passion is for the Adult Literacy program which teaches adults who have never had the chance to go to school and gives them a world of new opportunities to transform their family tree. Each student is taught reading and math to a fifth grade level which makes them *eligible for government employment. They are taught basic hygiene, income earning trade skills, and budgeting. They are also introduced to the Gospel message through their Christian teachers and tutors. About 30% of the students give their life to Christ in the first year. Seeds of the Gospel have been planted in the others hopefully for harvest at a later date. We now give to the Literacy program, $30 per month, which is what it costs to educate one student each month.*

Living a generous life brings joy. God has given us everything and you should give out of gratitude for what He has given to you. You need to find your passion, whether that be Organization Name or somewhere else. I pray you and your family find where to support.

Please call if you have any more questions. xxx-xxx-xxxx

Patti

What a great answer! Patti starts the reply by acknowledging my question and complimenting me for asking it. She acknowledges that I must have spent some time on the website and points me to further information before diving into a story. And what a story it is! Patti tells me why she is passionate about the organization and how she came to work there. She demonstrates through story her passion for India (the focus of this particular organization) and successfully allows me to see the organization through a donor's eyes, further moving me down the path to seeing myself as a donor. You'll notice at the end of the case to support the organization she says this line, "We now give to the Literacy program, $30 per month, which is what it costs to educate one student each month." She is building a case for me to become a continuity donor. She backs up the case for their work with results, and in the final paragraph, she addresses the part of my question about giving to a competitor or not at all.

Patti also gives me her phone number in case I have follow up questions, and she signs the email with her name (last name omitted for anonymity).

Though several organizations provided good responses, there was a disparity between the "excellent" responses and the "inadequate" or "poor" responses. In other words, if the organization responded, it was either a great response or a very poor one.

Use this simple test to check on your organization. Have a friend send an email and a Facebook message with this question, and see how your nonprofit responds (if at all). The response may surprise you!

After discovering that so many nonprofit organizations struggle with adequately explaining their case for support with a potential donor, I decided to continue my search for why donors support nonprofits.

I designed a study consisting of nationwide (U.S.) donors 25 years old and older. The donors were selected across a wide variety of nonprofits to determine which characteristic motivated them to donate to the specific organization. The survey questions were open-ended, so similar answers were grouped. I surveyed 300 donors in this study.

Several important themes that came out of the survey to examine. The first was that trustworthiness is a primary driver for donors. What the study doesn't answer is how exactly an organization builds trust with the donor.

The second takeaway was that affinity is a strong attraction for donors. Donors who have been impacted by a cause personally, whether through a friend or a relative, are more likely to support an organization working to solve that problem. For example, someone who's mom survived cancer is likely to support an organization pledging to fight cancer.

Finally, the survey showed that though a few key characteristics were frequently answered, there are a variety of reasons why someone chooses to support an organization, from religious to simply being asked to give.

The research has shown there is something that separates nonprofits that successfully attract new donors, volunteers, and employees from those that don't. It isn't luck or happenstance. What separates these nonprofits is more deliberate. Though a particular nonprofit may not realize they're successfully practicing these habits, there are distinct characteristics that attractive nonprofits have over others. This list of characteristics is what separates a Magnetic Nonprofit from other nonprofit organizations.

A Magnetic Nonprofit is one that attracts the right people to become supporters and volunteers.

Essentially what I found from my research and the survey results is that the characteristics of attractive nonprofits are categorized into the six Ts of a Magnetic Nonprofit:

1. Transparency: Openly sharing information

2. Thankful: Shows gratitude

3. Tenured: Longevity of an organization or ability to project expertise

4. Timely: How quickly a nonprofit responds to an external situation or communications with donors and volunteers

5. Testimony: An affinity to a cause because of a personal experience or experience of someone closely connected to the donor

6. Tribe: People in your circle of support

These six characteristics apply not only to donors but also to employees and volunteers. When these six characteristics are perfectly aligned, your organization could enter into a supporter's "top three organizations." The top three organizations are the ones that come to mind first when someone wants to support a cause with resources such as time, money, or even working for the organization.

For some supporters, not all six characteristics will apply a strong magnetic pull. The interesting thing about becoming a Magnetic Nonprofit is your magnetism will have different levels of strength for different people. There is rarely an organization that has a strong magnetic field for all people. Instead, specific characteristics will have a stronger pull than others. However, when all six characteristics (or Ts) are strong with a particular supporter, your magnetic field will have a very strong effect on them.

It's important to note that the six Ts to becoming a Magnetic Nonprofit are not the donors' motivations to give. Donors may express a variety of reasons for donating from "because the organization asked" to "I feel good when I donate." Instead, becoming a Magnetic Nonprofit increases your ability to appeal to your target audience. People will be drawn to your organization to give, join your staff, or volunteer because the characteristics align with who they are. A Magnetic Nonprofit draws people in to support it because of how they're positioned, irrespective of the motivations of the donor.

HEART OF A DONOR STUDY

In the 2010 *Heart of a Donor: Insights into donor motivation and behaviors for the 21st century* study, Russ Reid, a fundraising agency, found that donors did the following activities before giving for the first time. I've labeled each activity with one of the six Ts that supports a Magnetic Nonprofit:

- Visited the organization's website (Transparency)

- Searched the Internet for news about the organization (Testimony)

- Talked to someone who supports the organization (Tribe)

- Checked the organization's website to find out how much is spent on overhead (Transparency)

- Checked a watchdog organization to find out the organization's rating (Transparency)

- Talked with an employee (Tribe)

- Read the organization's annual report (Transparency)

- Visited the organization in person (Transparency)

- Visited the organization's social media profiles (Tribe)

The *Heart of a Donor* study also found that trustworthiness, cause, and integrity were the top three descriptive terms donors use to describe their favorite organization. In the study, Reid found that the favorite organization across all donor demographics came at the intersection of personal relevance, donor experience, and organizational trustworthiness.

AN EXAMPLE

Let's look at a specific funnel I recently experienced when I became a new donor.

I learned about Pencils of Promise from a podcast I listen to weekly. Because I trust the podcast host (after listening to over 100 episodes), when he discussed Pencils of Promise, I decided to look into the organization. Also, because the podcast host is a part of my tribe, I was drawn to learn more.

I joined their email list and began receiving regular communication from the organization. The organization was timely in how they communicated with me and with the frequency of their appeals. I reviewed their annual report and financials, and I found the organization had a high level of transparency with the information they shared.

When I perused their site, I learned Pencils of Promise was founded in 2008, telling me the organization is tenured and has about a decade of work to support their mission. The founder, Adam Braun, wrote a book, so I purchased it and discovered that I could relate to his passion for lifting people out of poverty (Testimony).

All of these characteristics produced a magnetic field strong enough for me to trust the organization. Trusting the organization resulted in a donation.

After my donation, I received a well-written thank-you note. Thankfulness contributes to becoming a lifelong donor.

Not every giving funnel will proceed the same way. You may be spontaneously motivated at an event to sponsor a child, or you may receive a direct mail letter and be motivated to give without feeling a magnetic pull from all six characteristics. As an organization, it's beneficial to have donor acquisition that doesn't require all six characteristics to be present before someone donates. However, to get the second gift and beyond, you must start a donor down a journey where s/he feels a strong magnetic field from these six traits. Though you may never achieve all six with a particular donor, if you can relate in just a few areas and build trust, you'll find yourself as one of the donor's top three organizations that s/he supports.

THE SIX TS TO BECOME A MAGNETIC NONPROFIT

Now let's briefly explore each of the six Ts that lead to becoming a Magnetic Nonprofit.

There are three groups of attributes of a Magnetic Nonprofit: Active, Assigned, and Individualistic. Each of the six attributes fits inside a specific group.

Active

Active attributes are ones that a nonprofit organization can address by acting. An organization can change these attributes by creating a plan and changing how the organization does something.

Active magnetic attributes are Transparency and Thankful.

For many donors, volunteers, and employees, transparency is the key to winning their support. These supporters want easy access to your financial data and an understanding of how you do your work – a transparent nonprofit shares this information in a way that is easy to absorb and act on.

Putting transparency into practice at your nonprofit increases trust and attracts new supporters. People want to give, but they need to know where their money is going and if your organization will use the gift most effectively. Many younger givers are moving away from efficiency as the primary attribute that motivates their giving. They are now looking for organizations that are hyper-transparent.

Team Rubicon, a disaster relief nonprofit working with veterans, reveals internal documents through its Open initiative.[2] Anyone can review stats from the organization and action reports from disasters responded to, and learn how the organization operates. This kind of transparency builds trust with potential donors.

Against Malaria takes transparency to a new level by detailing every single donation the organization receives and how each gift was used[3]. The organization also reveals precisely how many mosquito nets are distributed and where they went, how the organization makes decisions, and shares all of their financials in various levels of presentation from detailed to "easier to understand."

Recently, Fidelity Charitable found that 81% of donors are concerned about nonprofit transparency[4] and understanding the impact of their giving.

Donors are demanding transparency and we need to respond.

Building transparency into how you operate creates opportunities for your organization to be attractive for a considerable number of donors and volunteers.

---

[2] https://teamrubiconusa.org/open/
[3] https://www.againstmalaria.com/Donations.aspx
[4] https://www.fidelitycharitable.org/docs/overcoming-barriers-to-giving.pdf

The second active magnetic attribute is thankful. A thankful nonprofit shows gratitude to its donors, volunteers, and staff.

Multiple studies have shown the benefits of gratitude[5]. Gratitude will:

- Make us happier

- Create a connection where people like us

- Produce a healthier life

- Boost our career

- Strengthen our emotions

- Develop our personality

- Make us more optimistic

- Reduce materialism

- Increase spiritualism

- Make us less self-centered

---

[5] https://www.happierhuman.com/benefits-of-gratitude/

- Increase our self-esteem

- Improve our sleep

- Help us live longer

- Increase energy levels

- Make us feel good

- Make our memories happier

- Improve our decision-making

Studies have shown that when someone shows us gratitude, it provides a feedback loop where we feel more thankful. This gratitude results in the list above and many more positive feelings.

In the *Heart of a Donor Study*, the results demonstrate why it's vital to thank donors. A question was asked regarding what organizations have done to encourage donors to support the organization again. Seventy-two percent of the respondents stated the organization made them feel that the gift really made a difference, and 71% of the respondents said the organization gave them information about exactly what the gift helped accomplish. Demonstrating gratitude after receiving a gift will help over 70% of your donors be attracted to your organization.

Assigned

Assigned magnetic attributes are ones determined by how someone views the organization. A nonprofit organization can improve magnetism in these areas by working to change the supporter's impression of the organization.

The two magnetic attributes that are assigned by people are tenure and timely.

SOS SAHEL is an African-born organization with over 40 years of experience providing food security and nutrition training to rural communities in Sub-Saharan Africa. In 2017, during the week surrounding Africa Day, May 25, the organization invited more than 250 guests to a learning and celebration event. The event began with a gala. Throughout the week, guests also visited a pilot farm and dairy plant, both developed by SOS SAHEL as a part of its mission.

SOS SAHEL has been successful for four decades because of high-quality programs and a commitment to tell the stories of their work. This magnetic organization is tenured.

Tenure can be a strong force for donors to be attracted to an organization. In the donor's mind, the longer an organization has been around can be extrapolated to assume the organization will be around for some time. A donor wants her gift to go to a stable organization.

Tenure isn't limited to the number of years your organization has been in existence. For a donor, tenure can also be driven by the stories you tell, thought leadership, and partnerships.

The stories you tell impact how a donor views your organization. When you tell stories with successful outcomes and demonstrate how donors can make a difference, it can form a view in the donor's mind of the authority of your organization. Think of Charity: water. Though the organization is relatively young (founded in 2006), in many donors' minds it is the authority on clean water. By leading with strong storytelling, Charity: water has cemented itself as a tenured clean water nonprofit.

Secondly, tenure can be driven by your thought leadership. Wikipedia defines 'thought leader' as "an individual or firm that is recognized as an authority in a specialized field and whose expertise is sought and often rewarded."[6] Thought leadership can come from your internal program staff, executive leadership, or external experts who endorse your work. When a donor sees content that demonstrates your thought leadership and tenure is an important attribute to him, he registers the expertise as a positive for your organization.

---

[6] https://en.wikipedia.org/wiki/Thought_leader

Finally, partnerships can lend credibility to your organization. A collaboration with another organization, a corporation, a government agency, or an influencer can lend credibility and a belief of tenure with a potential donor. The donor sees a partner they trust and thinks, "if a government agency of this stature trusts this nonprofit, I can trust them, too." Though your organization may not have a long tenure in calendar terms, demonstrating expertise and experience with trusted partners will build your credibility.

The second assigned magnetic attribute is timely.

In October 2016, Hurricane Matthew struck Haiti, causing almost $2 billion in damage. About three weeks after the hurricane, I received an email appeal from a relief organization we support. This was the first appeal I saw from them for Hurricane Matthew, while most of the other organizations we support sent appeals just days after the hurricane struck.

Several years ago, with a different organization, I completed a request for information about becoming a volunteer. Months went by, and I forgot about the card I filled out. Then I received a letter in the mail with volunteer opportunities. I had received no communication from the organization in the months between filling out the card and the first letter I received.

These two examples demonstrate why it's vital for an organization to be timely with their communications. In the first example, appealing weeks after a disaster, in what I perceived as the first time the organization asked for money for this disaster, is not only poor fundraising practice, but it also makes me question whether or not the organization is paying attention. In the second example, even if the organization had no current volunteer opportunities, they should have been timelier with communications to keep the potential volunteer audience "warm" until the organization needed volunteers.

A timely nonprofit organization communicates with donors, volunteers, and employees at the right times. It doesn't mean the organization has to be the quickest in sending out communications. Sometimes pausing to consider how to communicate something is the right strategy. It does mean that the organization communicates in the right amount of time for the right audience. A timely organization understands the need for urgency in its work and fundraising.

Individualistic

Individualistic magnetic attributes are ones that are determined at an individual level. These are attributes that are decided by a supporter's history, beliefs, interactions, and passions for specific causes. For these attributes, the organization's role is to publicize the specific cause it's involved in to the right audiences. The two magnetic attributes that are individualistic are testimony and tribe.

My grandfather was a Brigadier General in the Ohio National Guard. Both of my parents also served in the Ohio National Guard, along with my brother and numerous aunts, uncles, and cousins. Therefore, I feel connected to an organization that helps serve our military service members, veterans, and their families.

Two decades ago, I visited Haiti on a mission trip to build a playground at a hospital for orphans and refurbish part of the facility. Ever since then, I've felt a connection to Haiti and support several organizations doing good work there.

You may have had cancer in your family, or lived through it yourself, and now have an affinity to support cancer-fighting organizations. Or perhaps you were adopted as a child, so now you support adoption agencies by volunteering your time.

Many of us give to organizations because of a personal connection, or because we have a testimony for a particular cause, country, or type of service. Testimony is a strong pull for people to support, volunteer, and work for a nonprofit organization. Organizations that communicate how effectively they accomplish work for a particular cause will draw in people who have this affinity of support.

World Relief is an international nonprofit organization working in relief, development, and with refugees. Each year, the local U.S. chapters of World Relief each hold a 5k race. Hundreds of people who are passionate about serving the most vulnerable participate in the 5k. Beyond the race, thousands of volunteers give time to World Relief to assist the organization and help with refugee placement. This core group of supporters belong to the same tribe: they want to serve refugees and other vulnerable people.

World Relief has discovered the secret to being a part of their supporters' tribe. The organization offers a value exchange for people to feel good about their support to volunteer for the organization.

In his book *Tribes: We Need You to Lead Us*, Seth Godin defines a tribe as a group of people connected to one another, connected to a leader, or connected to an idea. For millions of years, human beings have been part of one tribe or another. A group needs only two things to be a tribe: a shared interest and a way to communicate.

A tribe has boundaries. People have a psychological need for inclusion and exclusion. We need to feel like we are a part of something, but we need to feel like not everybody can be a part of it. It makes us feel special when we're a part of something that doesn't let everyone in. We also need a purpose for the tribe and something that we're fighting for/against.

For World Relief, supporters share a common desire to help refugees and fight against those seeking harm to these people. It's a powerful connection to the organization.

Now that you've learned about the six attributes of a Magnetic Nonprofit, let's explore why you should become one.

WHY SHOULD YOU BECOME A MAGNETIC NONPROFIT?

A Magnetic Nonprofit is one that attracts donors, volunteers, and staff. It operates within a framework of consistently speaking to the heart of these supporters. The Magnetic Nonprofit doesn't attract everybody, instead it attracts the *right* people. The right people are the ones who align with the six characteristics that make the nonprofit magnetic.

It's essential to understand this concept: the nonprofit doesn't need everybody, it just needs the right people to accomplish its mission and achieve its vision.

A Magnetic Nonprofit attracts new donors to the cause and motivates existing donors to continue giving. The characteristics of a Magnetic Nonprofit help people move down the supporter funnel to become donors by enabling them to know, like, and trust the organization. For example, when an organization is transparent with its finances, it helps build trust. Likewise, when someone is a member of a tribe, he is more likely to prefer organizations that others in his tribe like.

Volunteers feel good when they support a Magnetic Nonprofit. The same characteristics that motivate someone to give also help them decide to volunteer with an organization by donating their time. People volunteer for many reasons, such as altruism, because it makes them feel good, so they can meet people, learn new skills, or just to have fun.

HOW CAN YOUR ORGANIZATION BECOME A MAGNETIC NONPROFIT?

It's not ok that your organization doesn't have the funding you need. It's not ok you're losing donors. It's not ok that you're struggling to find volunteers and staff.

You can attract the right donors, volunteers, and staff.

To develop this magnetism, you'll need to understand the different ways a nonprofit can attract people. These six attributes need to be personal to the supporter, something the nonprofit can realistically attain, and bring in the right donors, volunteers, and staff.

Before describing each attribute of magnetism, let's learn what may be holding back your organization's growth and success. In other words: barriers to magnetism.

Barriers to Magnetism

One of the fascinating scientific characteristics of a true magnetic field is that there aren't many physical materials that can block a strong magnetic field. There isn't an equivalent to an electric insulator. Instead, when attempting to block a magnetic field, you must use a material that is either thick enough or made of certain physical properties, so the magnetic field won't be strong enough to reach through.

Essentially, if your magnetism is very strong, it's hard to block — regardless of "material" or "thickness." Or in this case, barriers.

By their nature, donors, staff, and supporters who are passionate about your cause don't build strong barriers. They aren't consciously designing a way to fend off your organization. Instead, the psychological mechanisms they use to decide if your organization is worthy of their support are weak barriers. If you aren't attracting donors, staff, or supporters, it's because your magnetism isn't strong enough.

What can affect the strength of your magnetism? Let's explore the seven areas that can reduce a magnetic field:

1. The way it's always been

2. Inward focus

3. Leadership buy-in

4. Staff scalability

5. Infrastructure scalability

6. Knowledge gap

7. Criminal or unethical behavior

THE WAY IT'S ALWAYS BEEN

"I'd like to change the Easter appeal," Jack, the new development director at a 14-year-old nonprofit, explained to his development team. "Looking at the results, we've been sending this same appeal year after year for some time and results have been dwindling."

"But we've always sent the same Easter appeal; our donors like it," Julie, the direct marketing manager, explained. "I don't think we should change something that's a foundation of our fundraising efforts."

Jack replied, "It's obvious from the results that the *donors* don't like it. They're not giving to it. Perhaps our staff is in love with this particular appeal, but they aren't the ones taking action on it."

The first barrier to magnetism is repeating the same mistakes over and over again just because this is how it's always been done.

A nonprofit leader's role is to create a Magnetic Nonprofit that draws in new supporters, reinforces relationships with existing donors, attracts the best employees, and brings in new volunteers. This will inevitably lead to necessary change, and this is when the "this is the way we've always done things around here" will rear its ugly head. This isn't unique to nonprofits. Many organizations suffer from this syndrome that refuses to allow for positive change. You must break through this barrier to become a Magnetic Nonprofit.

In the example above, Jack identified a situation where the organization hasn't refreshed a failing appeal because it's how it's always been done. If you want to create and maintain a Magnetic Nonprofit, you'll need to start letting data and results guide your decisions. There's an applicable saying that's helpful to remember: don't bring an opinion to a data fight. If the data is telling you it's time for a change, be willing to change.

A good illustration of this concept is the business fable about the gorillas. The origins of this fable are unknown.

Imagine you placed five gorillas into a cage. In the middle of the cage, you hang a bunch of bananas above a ladder. When a gorilla starts to climb the ladder to get the bananas, you spray all of the gorillas with cold water until they retreat to the corners of the cage. When another gorilla attempts to get the bananas, you spray them all with cold water again.

After a short time, if a gorilla attempts to climb the ladder to get the bananas, the other gorillas will stop him, not wanting to be sprayed with cold water.

Now if you remove a single gorilla and replace him with a new gorilla and the new gorilla attempts to climb the ladder to get the bananas, the original four gorillas will stop him from pursuing the bananas. As you replace each gorilla with a new gorilla, the remaining four gorillas will stop the new gorilla from trying to reach the bananas.

As you replace the last gorilla with a new gorilla, the four gorillas who have never experienced being sprayed with cold water will continue to stop the new gorilla from trying to reach the bananas. Now, with five gorillas who have never been sprayed with cold water, none of them will try to reach the bananas. Why? Because that's the way it's always been done.

You must overcome this attitude with your staff and continually question how you do things. This will keep your processes fresh and allow you to innovate.

Embrace the history and learnings you've experienced as a nonprofit.

When your experience feeds your current marketing and fundraising strategies and doesn't blindly require them to follow tradition, you will no longer experience the "this is the way we've always done things around here." Instead, you're using your experience to make educated decisions. Making informed decisions helps you become a Magnetic Nonprofit.

INWARD FOCUS

I received an email appeal a year ago from a local community service organization I've supported in the past. This organization does good work, especially in caring for homeless veterans and single mothers. A noticeable shift in their messaging had occurred over the course of about 18 months. The most recent appeal I received was focused entirely on the accomplishments of the organization and didn't speak to me as a donor. It no longer explained or showed the impact of my financial contributions. The email solicited a donation, so I clicked through to the landing page and read a short story about the organization with no clear way to donate. The only way I found to give was to go through the standard navigation at the top of the page and click through two more pages before finally finding a way to donate!

The convoluted landing page was a grievous "sin" in fundraising, but the organization also introduced a barrier for my continued support: inward focus. An organization becomes inwardly-focused when most of the copy talks about the organization and there are too few words talking about the donor. When the organization becomes the hero, the donor loses interest.

Here's an example of an inwardly-focused appeal. I masked the organization's name and certain appeal details, calling the organization "HopeMedz."

Help HopeMedz Provide Urgent Disaster Relief Today!

Hurricane John has devastated the Dominican Republic and threatens people in south Florida. HopeMedz is on-site providing medical kits and emergency supplies.

Your gift will allow HopeMedz to restock emergency medical relief and other supplies to help those impacted by these hurricanes. HopeMedz is saving lives!

Please give generously so we can continue our good work and provide for those devastated by disaster.

- *HopeMedz has provided over 1,000 disaster kits through partners in the Dominican Republic.*

- *HopeMedz is shipping 500 water filters to provide clean water to those impacted.*

"When I saw the destruction brought by Hurricane John, I knew HopeMedz had to step in to help save lives. I'm so proud of our people on the ground distributing disaster kits and saving lives," said David Smith, President of HopeMedz.

Please give generously today to enable HopeMedz to continue saving lives!

It's easy to spot an inwardly-focused organization. The communication pieces contain a lot of "we" and "I" verbiage and less "you" and "your" language.

In donor communications, there is a concept of positioning the *donor as the hero*. The hero of a story is the one who drives the story. Your nonprofit is simply the guide helping the donor accomplish his/her goal: to help people s/he has a passion for helping. When you position the organization as the hero, and not the donor, s/he won't make that connection that your organization can be the tool s/he wants to use to make a difference.

In the HopeMedz example, you can make some small changes that will resonate well with readers:

Help Provide Urgent Disaster Relief Today!

Hurricane John has devastated the Dominican Republic and threatens people in south Florida. You can save lives today by providing medical kits and emergency supplies.

Your gift will restock emergency medical relief and other supplies to help those impacted by these hurricanes TODAY. You are saving lives!

Please give generously to continue the good work and provide for those devastated by disaster.

- *Donors like you have provided over 1,000 disaster kits through partners in the Dominican Republic – but there's more work needed to be done.*

- *HopeMedz is shipping 500 water filters to provide clean water to those impacted.*

"When I saw the destruction brought by Hurricane John, I immediately thought of you, our faithful donors, who have a heart to step in to help save lives. Thank you for distributing disaster kits and saving lives," said David Smith, President of HopeMedz.

Please give generously today to continue saving lives!

Change "I" and "we" language into "you" language to create an appeal that attracts donors.

Donor-focused language doesn't end with fundraising appeals. Review your communication copy, newsletters, website, and thank-you letters, and count how many times you use "we" or "I" in the text. Rewrite the pieces so they use "you" and "your" to position the donor as the one making a difference. For example, you may have a line like this in your annual report:

In the previous year, we helped 2,500 families receive clean water by building wells!

You can rewrite this line to position the line as a success because of the donor:

In the previous year, you helped us build wells so 2,500 families could receive clean water!

This simple change of verbiage to be from the donor's perspective will completely shift the donor's thinking from *"that's a good organization doing good work"* to *"that's a good organization that I can use to do good work."* This shift translates into more donors and volunteers.

LEADERSHIP BUY-IN

The third barrier to magnetism is leadership buy-in. Usually, this isn't caused by a leader sabotaging the efforts of an organization becoming more magnetic, but instead the leader believes s/he is doing the right thing. When s/he doesn't recognize that his/her actions or beliefs are hurting attracting new supporters, it can become a barrier for your organization to achieve your goals or accomplish your vision.

I have a colleague, Anne, who worked for a medium-sized nonprofit several years ago. A few weeks into her new job as a development manager, she began seeing tactics that could create a negative impression with donors. She brought them to the attention of her leadership team and they dismissed her concerns. Anne knew it needed to change. So, she set out to change their minds. Anne followed these steps:

First, Anne listened to her leadership. She discovered what they did and didn't value. At this organization, the management team wanted to maximize major donor lifetime value, but they were okay with some tactics to maximize short-term lifts in revenue from mass donors. Her boss's goals and definition of success were almost entirely aligned with the department's quarterly revenue growth.

Second, Anne identified someone on the leadership team that would champion her ideas. Anne wanted to instill a donor-centric view to fundraising and reduce the number of digital appeals donors received. The organization was sending up to 12 email appeals each month to specific segments, with zero non-ask emails. A non-ask email is one that is sent to build relationship with donors without asking for money.

Third, Anne met with the potential champion to hear the champion's views and ideas on fundraising. She learned how the leadership team built the revenue budget and the importance of the short revenue maximization. She listened and asked just a few questions.

Fourth, Anne developed a proposal to run a small test with a specified group of donors to see if she could change the frequency of fundraising emails, add impact reporting, and increase their giving in the fiscal year.

Fifth, she sought feedback from the champion before presenting it to more of the leadership team. She incorporated this feedback and made her case to the fundraising leadership.

Sixth, she had to be willing to compromise on some of the elements of her plan. The tweaks didn't impact the overall goal, so Anne accepted their feedback and received permission to test a group of donors.

Seventh, she reported back the results to the leadership team. In this case, she found statistical evidence that her proposed email frequency and mix lifted revenue over 15% in three months. She also saw donor attrition decrease — the organization kept more of its donors!

The organization shifted its communications plan to the one proposed by Anne.

Anne understood that leadership buy-in is crucial for the organization to move to become more magnetic. Leaders must see the value (and success) in becoming more attractive to supporters.

STAFF SCALABILITY

Your organization's staff can be a barrier to becoming a magnetic organization. If you have staff who are against change or don't understand why you need to transform your organization, they may consistently put up roadblocks as you try to become more magnetic.

Let's explore different types of staff at your organization.

First, there are staff members who work at your nonprofit **solely for the income**. They may have an affinity for the cause or say the right words, but they are there to earn a paycheck. When the going gets tough, these individuals head for greener pastures. Some of these staff members may be the easiest to move to a Magnetic Nonprofit mindset, as they are there for the paycheck and will do as instructed. Others will resist, believing their job may be in jeopardy, out of fear of change, or only because you're moving them out of their comfort zone. Since these staff members are less motivated by the cause, and more by the reward, you should explain how continued growth for your organization means increased salaries and job opportunities.

Second, there are staff members who are at your nonprofit because they **believe in the cause but are not necessarily in the right job**. These staff members are hired into a role that may not be the perfect fit, but they are not there for the career. They are there to fight for justice! These staff members want the organization to be successful because they have a heart for the people you serve. These employees are motivated by the progress towards your cause. With these staff members, explain how creating a Magnetic Nonprofit attracts more donors and volunteers, allowing you to get more good work accomplished. Your goal as a nonprofit leader should be to move these individuals into their best fit within the organization.

Not finding the right spot for staff can hold you back. For example, if you have a staff member who has been with the organization for eight years and moved from an accounting assistant to a web developer because s/he "likes tinkering with websites," s/he may not be positioned for success. If s/he has the right attitude and aptitude and is willing to learn, perhaps there will be a good outcome. If instead, s/he is passionate about the cause but is a poor web developer, you need to make the tough decision to find a better position or replace him/her with a web developer who is qualified *and* passionate about the cause.

Third, there are staff members that **believe in the cause *and* are in the right position** for their skill set, education, and experience. These individuals are in the right spot and believe in the cause. These staff members may still be a barrier to magnetism if they don't buy into your strategic transformation. Explaining the benefits of becoming more magnetic will help move these staff members to contribute and not remain a barrier.

Let me give you a warning about staff obstructions. Some staff members are at your organization because they love working at a nonprofit and they are actively trying to mold the nonprofit into their image for the organization. Staff members who are actively trying to move the organization to their vision for what they believe you should be doing are detrimental to the cause and the organization's health. They breed mistrust as they actively work toward what *they* want and not what's best for the team and organization as a whole. You will need to harness their desire to help and move them towards the organization's vision and mission, or you'll need to let them go.

Staff can become a barrier to transforming your organization into a magnetic one. With the right coaching and communication, you can move the right individuals into the right positions and help them understand the benefits of becoming a Magnetic Nonprofit.

INFRASTRUCTURE SCALABILITY

Your organization's infrastructure can be a barrier to becoming a Magnetic Nonprofit. When we look at the infrastructure of an organization, we see that it is composed of systems.

A system is a procedure, process, method, or course of action designed to achieve a specific result. Its parts and interrelated steps work together for the good of the whole. Creating effective business systems is the only way to attain results that are consistent, measurable, and that ultimately benefit donors and staff.

Michael Gerber, author of *eMyth*, said, "Organize around business functions, not people. Build systems within each business function. Let systems run the business and people run the systems. People come and go but the systems remain constant."

Typical systems include new donor acquisition, accounts payable, payroll, donation processing, direct mail fundraising, opening a new field office, food delivery, building a new well, information systems, and hiring. When you have healthy, well-defined, and well-executed systems, your organization is better prepared for growth. When your systems aren't healthy, you experience delays, mistakes are made, people don't understand what the next step is, you overpay for things, your efficiency declines, staff is unhappy, and you don't report back results to your donors in a timely fashion.

A healthy system takes time to design and deploy. It also requires you to measure results and make changes for improvement. There is no perfect system. You should continuously improve your systems.

Here's an example. Food for the Hungry's donation management system was unable to print custom receipts for donors based on what they gave to. Every donor received the same receipt, but we wanted more personalization to create a better donor experience. We identified what the problems were in the system and set out to design a fix. It wasn't easy — or fast. It took over two years to identify and develop a solution for custom receipting.

We had a broken system. We created a solution to remove a barrier that improved our timeliness and gratitude.

First, we identified what the problem was. In this example, the broken system was printing a homogenized donation receipt and not delivering it in a timely fashion. Know that it may take some time to discover all of the elements that are impacted by the desired change.

Next, we wrote down the desired system outcome and the process that would deliver it. We wanted a functioning system where personalized donation receipts are printed for each donor and delivered in a timely fashion. Documenting the new system will help identify areas where you might miss something. There could be decision points that impact system development. For example, how would we receipt monthly donors? If someone gave to ten different areas, what would that receipt look like? Would we send receipts to major donors or have their assigned representatives handwrite thank-you notes? How would we communicate that a major donor gave to their rep? As you brainstorm all the different ways a system could go, document it with a flow chart that shows each step in the system.

Third, we identified what resources would be required to build the system. In our case, one of the delays was that the needed changes required our vendor to make significant changes to *their* system. You're not always going to be able to control the timing of the change. It's imperative to build a realistic timeline to change your system.

Next, we began changing the system to meet our newly-defined system. Though this may be the most time-consuming part of the system change, if you've correctly planned the change, it can be a smooth process. If you do run into problems, and you likely will, identify the change required and how it will impact system design. Part of the reason our change required two years is the dependency of some modules and their upgrade schedule. The vendor had a planned upgrade timeline and a few of the modules that required upgrades for custom receipting weren't ready. The project was on hold, as we waited on the vendor during that time.

Fifth, we tested and deployed the new system. Always test your system before deployment, even if it's not a technology system. For example, if you create a new system for donor acquisition, you'll want to test it to make sure you've identified and successfully addressed every step.

Finally, we measured the impact and made changes as required for continuous improvement. The first personalized receipts covered the primary donation areas. Next, we rolled out the new system to monthly givers. Finally, we moved all types of giving into the new system with personalized receipts.

Though your infrastructure may currently be a barrier to magnetism, by identifying the problems and creating or modifying systems, you'll reduce the barriers of becoming a Magnetic Nonprofit.

KNOWLEDGE GAP

The knowledge gap of what you know and communicate as a nonprofit compared to what the donor understands, can be a barrier to becoming a Magnetic Nonprofit.

Consider this website copy from Africare, a nonprofit building sustainable communities in Africa:

Give someone a fish or teach someone to fish? Africare comes down firmly on the "teach" side of the question. Development projects are only truly successful if project participants gain knowledge in the process. Clothes get worn, food gets eaten and money gets spent. But knowledge gets passed on. If you really want to invest in Africa's future, invest in an African community's skills to control their own future.

From our mentorship approach to our substantial partnerships with local Civil Society Organizations, a description of practically every Africare project includes the phrases "knowledge transfer" or "sustainability." In practice, these phrases mean things like partnering with government agriculture extension workers on introducing new farming techniques on demonstration plots, training local masons to maintain household latrines, educating leaders to stress the importance of continued entrepreneurial training, equipping local institutions to deliver successful vocational training, empowering women to teach their sisters and mothers improved food preparation techniques, and the list goes on. Africare's goal is to support communities in achieving self-reliance, because then, and only then, can they achieve prosperity on their own terms.[7]

As an employee at a nonprofit, you understand your core work and programs at a level 9 or 10. The donor doesn't have this level of understanding. So, as a nonprofit marketer, you might try to communicate with the donor at a level 5 or 6. The problem is, realistically your donor only understands your work at a level 1 or 2. The gap between how your nonprofit communicates with a supporter is known as the *knowledge gap.*

If you make assumptions about a supporter's understanding of how your nonprofit works and communicate to the supporter at too high of a level, you'll begin to lose magnetism. Communicating at too high of a level reduces transparency and trustworthiness with the donor.

If the supporter doesn't understand how you communicate, s/he will assume you're not transparent. Losing transparency reduces the ability for the donor to do more research into your organization, understand what you're doing, and believe that his/her support is necessary.

Your supporter may also begin to question the trustworthiness of your organization. If s/he doesn't

---

[7] https://www.africare.org/africares-approach/capacity-building/

understand what you're saying or believes you're hiding information, trust begins to erode. If the supporter can't trust the organization, s/he won't give.

Reduce the knowledge gap by communicating at the level of the intended audience. Don't use industry jargon or unfamiliar acronyms. Lower the "education level" of your content to speak at a level that is more universally understood. For most nonprofits, public-facing communications should have a 6th through 8th-grade readability level. You can use a tool like HemingwayApp.com to "grade" your content's reading level.

The example above from Africare is written at a grade level 16! The readability of the description of the organization's work is best suited for a college graduate, not a sixth-grader.

Communicating at a sixth-grade level doesn't mean "dumbing down" your content. It takes high intelligence to write about complex topics at a simpler level! Instead, writing for grade 6-8 levels of education allows you to communicate your organization's work at a universal level. At this level, your supporter will intuitively understand your work and better understand how s/he can be a part of it.

The knowledge gap also applies to volunteers. Many volunteers have a desire to help but lack the specific technical skills related to your nonprofit. Design training systems to help onboard volunteers, so they don't feel inadequate when they show up to help.

Similarly, when a new staff member joins your organization, s/he may have the necessary technical expertise but do not yet understand the institutional knowledge. If your organization is anything like Food for the Hungry, you likely have a lot of acronyms and jargon. Take time to provide the foundational training to new staff regarding your vision, mission, values, purpose, programmatic model, locations, and strategic plan. Foundational training helps a new team member feel more confident in their role.

CRIMINAL BEHAVIOR

An iron object can be magnetized so it can attract metal. When something is magnetized, it's placed within a strong magnetic field and the magnetic field is built with strength and polarity, all pointing in one direction. Conversely, when an iron tool is demagnetized, it is placed within a strong magnetic field where the strength and polarity alternates in different directions. The barriers we discussed were for an organization to have sufficient magnetic field strength. Alternatively, an organization could potentially become demagnetized altogether and no longer attract donors, employees, and volunteers.

Far too often, a minority of nonprofit organizations, or to be specific, leaders within those organizations, decide to break the law and use the resources of the nonprofit for their benefit. Stealing public money and using it for yourself is not only criminal behavior, but it also demagnetizes the organization and impacts far too many innocent lives from staff to beneficiaries.

In 2016, the National Children's Leukemia Foundation (NCLF) was shut down by the Attorney General of New York as a part of a settlement of a lawsuit alleging the NCLF repeatedly lied to donors about the extent of its charitable programs and that they falsified official filings. Of the $9.7 million in donations received from 2009 to 2013, only $57,541 was used to help beneficiaries. The organization made false statements on the website to entice donors to give, pretended to have a functioning board of directors, and guaranteed a lifetime pension of over $100,000 a year to its founder. As a part of the settlement, the officers were banned from serving as fiduciaries of any charity.

Organizations like NCLF have a demagnetizing effect on legitimate charities, as they have to convince donors who were cheated that they are trustworthy organizations.

Building a Magnetic Nonprofit will help build trust in the system and demonstrate to the public that nonprofits are transparent and trustworthy.

In the rest of this book, I'll show you how to create a Magnetic Nonprofit that attracts donors, volunteers, and staff.

TAKE ACTION

1) Go to http://magneticnonprofit.com/barriers for a free action worksheet.

2) Identify barriers to magnetism in your nonprofit.

3) Prioritize barrier removal.

4) Develop an action plan for each identified barrier.

Attribute One: Transparency

The American Legacy Foundation has received millions of dollars from the government's settlement with tobacco companies. The foundation prided itself on its research and telling the truth about the effects of smoking. Unfortunately, the organization suffered from a lack of transparency.

In 2011, the American Legacy Foundation completed a federal disclosure form and revealed the organization became aware of a diversion "in excess of $250,000 committed by a former employee."

The organization felt it had now met its disclosure requirements and didn't provide any additional information until investigative reporters did their own digging.

The press discovered that a former employee defrauded the organization of over $3.4 million. Fraudulent purchase orders were executed from a variety of false companies by an assistant vice president who now resides in Nigeria (I can't make this stuff up!).

American Legacy Foundation waited three years to reveal the fraud and didn't want to show the complete nature of what happened.

"We're not innocent in this," said American Legacy Chief Executive Cheryl Healton. "We are horrified it happened on our watch. . . . The truth hurts — we screwed up."

Unfortunately, what happened to American Legacy isn't rare. In a study performed by the Washington Post[8], over 1,000 charities disclosed a loss of $250,000 or more due to fraud between 2008 and 2012. This list included:

1. The 140-year-old Woodcock Foundation of Kentucky, an organization providing scholarships to the financially needy, disclosed alleged fraud by a former chairman who drained $1 million from the organization's accounts.

2. In 2009, Youth Service America discovered a former employee misappropriated $2 million. He was later sentenced to four years in prison for the theft.

3. The Maryland Legal Aid Bureau experienced a loss of at least $1.1 million, though officials believe it could be closer to $2.5 million.

4. The Miami Beach Community Health Center reported a $7 million loss in 2012 due to embezzlement by its former chief executive, who was later convicted of theft.

---

[8] https://www.washingtonpost.com/investigations/inside-the-hidden-world-of-thefts-scams-and-phantom-purchases-at-the-nations-nonprofits/2013/10/26/825a82ca-0c26-11e3-9941-6711ed662e71_story.html

The Internal Revenue Service reports that in 2009, nonprofit organizations revealed 285 diversions totaling $170 million.

All of these incidents hurt the nonprofit sector as a whole and make it more difficult for donors to trust. Transparency is one answer to helping build more trust with the public.

For many donors, volunteers, and employees, transparency is the key to winning their support. These supporters want easy access to your financial data and an understanding of how you do your work. A transparent nonprofit shares this information in a way that is easy to absorb and act on.

Let's explore nine ways to improve transparency:

1. Share openly and often.

2. Make your information easy to find.

3. Share your successes and failures.

4. Create firm policies.

5. Be honest in your fundraising.

6. Work with third-party rating agencies.

7. Freely share information with staff.

8. Provide a reporting mechanism.

9. Be open and transparent with institutions.

SHARE OPENLY AND OFTEN

You may believe your nonprofit is being transparent by posting audited financial statements and 990s, but the truth is — you're not doing enough.

Donors crave transparency from the nonprofit.

In the United States, nonprofit organizations are required by law to provide a certain level of financial transparency. They are required to disclose certain financial information upon request. However, nonprofit organizations should go above and beyond the legally-required standard to attract and gain the trust of new supporters.

Elevating your organization's level of transparency encourages people to trust your organization.

Additionally, employees also appreciate transparency and open communication that continues to build their trust in the organization.

Build trust by practicing transparency beyond the legal requirements.

A transparent organization is one that is willing to frequently and openly share results. To achieve this, your organization should always share information and post it on an easy-to-find page on your website. Food for the Hungry's financial page is consistently one of the top five most-visited pages on our website. People crave more information about your organization — give it to them.

PSI, a health services nonprofit, creates a monthly impact report. [9] This open access to its impact data and its performance helps keep supporters informed about what PSI is doing.

MAKE YOUR INFORMATION EASY TO FIND

Post your financial information, such as IRS form 990s, audited financial statements, and annual reports on your website.

Some nonprofits make it challenging to access this type of financial information. For example, some large nonprofit organizations require people to request their financial information or 990 forms in writing. Unnecessary barriers discourage people from supporting organizations because it makes them look less transparent.

List your board members and executive team on your website. When someone is interested in your organization, they research your website for more information. Providing a list of your board members and executive team with good bios helps people develop more confidence in your charity.

---

[9] https://www.psi.org/resource-type/data/

SHARE YOUR SUCCESSES AND FAILURES

A transparent organization not only shares a successful project campaign but also shares its failures.

Sharing failures is hard to do. None of us want to admit defeat.

It's counterintuitive — won't a potential supporter be discouraged when she reads about a failure? Some might, but many more will appreciate the honesty and transparency.

Each year, Engineers Without Borders (EWB), a Canadian nonprofit, creates a failure report alongside the organization's annual report. [10] In the report, the organization reveals the sector's fear of discussing failures:

We might lose donors. People might not want to invest in an organization that takes risks and the failures that may come.

However, EWB felt like the opportunity to learn from mistakes by highlighting failures leads to more dialogue about the challenges inherent in development work. The leadership team debated the risks involved in publicly documenting failures. They ultimately decided the opportunity to promote EWB's organizational culture of

---

[10] https://www.ewb.ca/en/about-us/governance/annual-report/

learning, humility, and transparency was too essential and outweighed the risk of losing support from funders.

In the years since, EWB has not lost a single donor or partner because of the Failure Report. Out of the failure report arose a second website, Admitting Failure[11], where organizations are encouraged to share their stories of failure.

CREATE FIRM POLICIES

Strong internal controls create a higher level of transparency for your nonprofit. Internal controls are policies, financial controls, and audits. Here are several policies your nonprofit should enact to promote transparency:

- **Conflict of interest**. A conflict of interest policy defines what constitutes an action or situation that creates a potential problem within the nonprofit. A conflict of interest policy requires staff or board members to disclose actual or potential conflict and prohibits people from acting in any matter in which there is a conflict.

- **Document retention/destruction**. Nonprofits produce many documents. Some have legal requirements for retention; others have a business

---

[11] https://www.admittingfailure.org

purpose for retention. Ensure you're following the law and creating transparency with your document retention policies.

- **Whistleblower protection**. A whistleblower is someone who discovers a problem (or potential problem) and reports the discovery. The nonprofit should have a whistleblower protection policy for staff to feel comfortable reporting a problem.

- **Gift acceptance**. In some circumstances, staff, leadership, and members of the board will be offered gifts from partners, governments, or other non-governmental organizations (NGOs). A gift acceptance policy defines what is acceptable.

- **Chapter, branch, and affiliate policies**. If a nonprofit has chapters, branches, or affiliates, how will they work together? A policy should be defined to describe this relationship. Will each individual chapter or affiliate have its own board and/or executive leadership? How will the organization file for organization structure with local governments? The policies should answer these questions.

- **Compensation setting procedures**. Executive compensation, usually the CEO or Executive Director, is set by the board of directors. The board should have a procedure for researching and setting executive compensation.

- **Debt collection**. Some nonprofits need to collect debts or payments from people, such as a hospital that needs to collect medical bills. What policies and guidelines will these nonprofits follow when collecting past due bills?

- **Restricted gifts**. Restricted gifts are ones that are designated for a specific purpose. When the organization raises more funds than needed for a restricted fund, what will happen to the overage? How will donor intent be honored?

- **Joint ventures**. From time to time, a nonprofit may partner with other nonprofits or for-profit corporations. A joint venture policy defines how the board or executive leadership team will consider joint venture partnerships and what constraints they should work under.

- **Investment and financial policies**. Investment policies dictate where and how nonprofits invest their funds. Adopt financial controls and management policies to reduce the chance someone could steal funds or resources, or commit other fraudulent activities at your organization.

The goal of these policies isn't to hamper the good work you do, but instead to ensure transparency and protection of donor gifts. Robust policies and procedures protect your staff, board, volunteers, leadership team, beneficiaries or participants, and donors. Review your policies at least once a year to confirm they are working as intended and are kept up to date with laws, regulations, and the current climate.

BE HONEST IN YOUR FUNDRAISING

Be honest and ethical in your fundraising. There are several situations where ethical issues may arise:

- **Tainted money**. For your organization, there are instances where you may not accept funds from certain corporations or individuals. For example, a gambling support organization wouldn't accept money from a casino. That same casino may donate to an art museum without issue.

- **Fundraising compensation based on a percentage of funds raised**. It may not be illegal, but it is unethical to pay a person raising funds based on a percentage of the funds raised. Fundraisers should be motivated by the mission, not by the compensation.

- **Messaging or photos that don't match the real situation**. Using messages or photos that don't match reality is unethical. Your fundraising appeal should match what is happening in the program you're funding. In other words, tell the truth. There are times where you must use purchased photography, such as in times of disaster appeals when you can't get media transmitted or in cases you cannot show the identity of a beneficiary. In these cases, properly attribute the photos to their source.

- **Targeting vulnerable donors**. Pressuring vulnerable donors who may not be able to afford to give should be avoided.

- **Donor privacy**. Once someone donates to your organization, it's your responsibility to ensure you keep the donor's data safe and private. Many companies want to buy donor data to resell to other organizations, sometimes unethically. Only collect the information you need and make sure you follow your privacy policies.

- **Communicate how funds are used**. A crucial part of the fundraising process is communicating how funds will be used and how they were used. Honest impact reporting helps a donor view your organization as transparent and trustworthy.

WORK WITH THIRD-PARTY RATING AGENCIES

Work with third-party rating agencies, like GuideStar (now Candid) or Charity Watchdog, to become a rated charity. Villanova University and the University of Wisconsin-Milwaukee found that nonprofits that earned the GuideStar Seal of Transparency averaged 53% more in contributions the following year than those that did not.

Many foundations use charity rating agencies as a trusted source for information before they give. Donors looking for highly-efficient charities also use these sources to find the best-rated charities to support.

FREELY SHARE INFORMATION WITH STAFF

There must be some separation of information between nonprofit leadership and the organization's staff, but many nonprofits err on the side of not sharing *enough* information. When you remain open with your employees, you'll find their trust in your leadership will rise — even if the information isn't good news.

Some time ago, I worked at a nonprofit that was going through a difficult financial period. During this time, the leadership team was open and honest about the financial situation and the steps taken to solve the problem. Not all of the steps were easy, but the staff, including myself, was grateful to the leadership team for trusting us with clear and honest communication.

When the going got tough, we came together as coworkers to help.

Contrast this with a mid-size nonprofit a friend of mine worked at as the manager of the human resources department. It was a constant struggle with the executive director to allow for information to be shared with the staff. Most employees didn't know the financial condition of the organization until the annual report was released. One year the organization was losing money, but the leadership didn't communicate the struggles until it was too late, and laid off 10% of the staff one Friday afternoon. The rest of the staff panicked and several key employees left the organization on their own. When you aren't openly sharing good and bad news, staff will fill in the gaps with their assumptions.

PROVIDE A REPORTING MECHANISM

Offer a mechanism for staff to feel safe to ask questions about transparency issues. The IRS requires nonprofits to answer the status of a "whistleblower policy" on the annual 990 forms. Nonprofits need to go beyond just offering a whistleblower policy and instead provide an anonymous reporting mechanism that ensures the confidentiality of the staff member.

BE OPEN AND TRANSPARENT WITH INSTITUTIONS

Being transparent also has an impact on foundation and institutional fundraising. For example, a South Boston church-based youth club offers a nursery, playgroups, computer and music classes, and other services to children regardless of their religion. A family foundation in Boston whose mission is to improve the quality of life of the deprived, disadvantaged, and excluded, was reticent to fund the youth club without seeing a reliable track record and impact reporting. Though the foundation didn't usually accept unsolicited grant applications, they were willing to work with the Priest that managed the youth club to explain how to attract funding.

The foundation suggested the youth club perform an independent organizational assessment to:

- Understand the context of the organizational effectiveness in a broader context of what services South Boston needs and what organization can supply those needs.

- Provide insight into the many activities that are already in place in the church and identify the need for more activities.

- Uncover the vision for the future of the youth club.

The organizational assessment led to a three-year relationship with the foundation. With a grant, the youth club was able to hire paid staff and expand its footprint in the community.

At smaller organizations, it can be difficult to expend the resources to go "above and beyond" for transparency. As this local youth club illustrates, being transparent can lead to great opportunities and growth for your nonprofit.

Putting transparency into practice at your nonprofit increases trust and attracts new supporters. People want to give, but they need to know where their money is going and if your organization will use the gift most effectively. Many younger givers are moving away from efficiency as the primary attribute that motivates their giving. They are now looking for organizations that are hyper-transparent.

TAKE ACTION

1) Audit your current policies and add any necessary ones to become more transparent.

2) Tell stories of your successes and failures.

3) Check your third-party ratings and update the information required to maintain a high rating.

4) Create a process to inform staff about organizational news and financial updates.

Attribute Two: Thankful

A key insight in the *Heart of a Donor Study* demonstrates why it's vital to thank donors. The study asked a question regarding what organizations have done to encourage donors to support the organization again. First, 72% of the respondents stated the organization made them feel that their gift made a difference. Second, 71% of the respondents said the organization gave them information about exactly what the gift helped accomplish. Properly demonstrating gratitude to donors will achieve both of these.

BEING A THANKFUL ORGANIZATION

What does it mean to be a thankful organization?

A thankful organization demonstrates gratitude in a variety of ways to donors, employees, and volunteers.

Whether you send a thank-you video, a note of gratitude, a welcome gift, a thank-you email, or another creative way to thank the donor for their donation, you need to communicate in a specific way to have the most significant impact on your donor. Sending your thanks is a pivotal way to continue developing the relationship with your donor. Appropriately expressing gratitude is a way to transform your donor file into a healthier one.

Most organizations are focusing their efforts on new donor acquisition strategies. How do we convert more donors in our acquisition mailing? Which Facebook Ad will result in a new donation? How do we acquire a continuity donor? How do we get more people to click the GIVE NOW button in our latest email?

For many of us working at nonprofit organizations, we work so hard to get that first gift, and it often happens that after the donor has given online or sent his/her check, s/he hears ... nothing. No thank-you note. No expression of gratitude. No explanation of the impact his/her gift made. Yes, s/he might receive an email receipt, but a s/he may not see that as a heartfelt demonstration of appreciation. The lack of expressing thanks "turns off" the donor and s/he moves on to give to another organization.

THANK THE DONOR

Merely thanking the donor is the best way to move the donor along the path towards a second gift, and ultimately to move your organization into the donor's top three. Improve your nonprofit fundraising by properly showing appreciation to your donor.

20-30% of the people who receive your thank-you communication will send back a gift. The bounce-back gifts can be a significant income for your nonprofit organization. We're not thanking people merely to win that next gift, but it's an integral part of the donor development process. Once you get people to give a second gift, the likelihood that they will continue giving to your organization rises.

Like all donor communications, there is a structure for thanking the donor that will have the most impact. First, your correspondence should be timely. Second, you need to demonstrate impact. Third, you should make the donor feel genuinely appreciated. Finally, communicate to your donor that they are the hero of the story.

BE TIMELY

On our first wedding anniversary, my wife and I pulled out a handful of thank-you cards that got missed when we sent out the batch from our wedding. We opened each one, wrote a short note of apology about why the card was late, resealed it, and sent it. We're sure people found humor in the situation but the recipients probably missed the appreciation.

Likewise, when we're not timely with our thank-you communication, you miss the opportunity to truly demonstrate your appreciation. Even a couple of weeks late will lose the luster of the communication. I recently donated to an organization and received my receipt a month later with no real note of gratitude. Receiving the receipt so late focused my attention on the lack of appreciation from the nonprofit organization.

You must be timely with your thank-you communication. Send your thanks as close to the donation as possible to have the maximum impact. This usually means sending it within 48 hours of the gift.

IMPACT REPORTING

It's easy to use industry jargon in our communications or generalize how the donor is helping. It doesn't contribute to the donor relationship to tell the donor the gift provided "hope." It would be best if you were more specific about the impact the donation made. Explaining the impact in the thank-you communication helps build trust with the donor that your organization will do good work with the gifts s/he makes.

What do I mean when I say "explain the impact"?

First, let's look at an example of a poorly worded thank-you I received.

"Your $35 donation for Emergency Response has been received. Your donation to Nonprofit Org, a 501c(3) tax-deductible organization, is tax-deductible as provided by law. Your donation is appreciated."

Tell a beneficiary story or provide a specific example of how the donor's gift will be used. For example, "Thank you for your $35 donation to our emergency response fund. Right now, we're rushing aid to refugees in the Middle East and your gift will help provide emergency supplies, food, and shelter for one family." You may not be able to tell the donor where her donation will be used explicitly, but you can give a general idea of the impact that she made.

Show your appreciation in *how* you thank the donor! This is not a receipt, nor should it be a form letter; this needs to be a personalized thank-you that demonstrates gratitude for the donation. A donor can smell a cookie-cutter message, so design something genuinely remarkable that sets your nonprofit apart.

Don't be over the top in your thanks in a way that the donor feels like it's cheesy or inauthentic. There's a line between being authentic and kissing up to the donor.

Write the thank-you messaging from the donor's point of view. The easy way to do this is to identify how many times you use "I" or "We" in the communication and rephrase it to use "you" and "your." Tell an emotional story with your thank-you, putting the donor into the position of being the driver of the good created by the donation. Here's an example thank-you communication:

We are so appreciative of your gift! We are helping lift people from poverty through our job training programs and placement services.

This is a good description of the work, but it's entirely from the point of view of the organization doing the good work! Place the donor into the story like this:

Your gift is making an immediate impact! You are helping lift people from poverty through job training programs and placement services.

It's a small change, but one that puts the donor into the story to demonstrate the good that s/he is doing. The donor is giving to you because s/he has a passion for the cause and you have the ability to impact change. You are the conduit by which s/he can make a positive impact. Let the donor feel like s/he deserves the credit for the excellent work.

CREATIVE WAYS TO THANK DONORS

The way you say thank-you to donors could be the most critical communication piece you have as a nonprofit organization. Unfortunately, many nonprofits send thank-you communications that read more like a formal tax receipt, rather than a heartfelt felt note of appreciation that motivates the donor to build a relationship with the organization.

It's much cheaper to build a relationship with an existing donor than to acquire a new one. In fact, this is key to healthy nonprofit fundraising. Let's explore creative ways to thank donors.

- **Send a heartfelt thank-you**. When you create a thank-you that is timely, explains the impact the donor made, and makes the donor feel truly appreciated, then you've created something relevant and meaningful to the donor. The heartfelt thank-you should be custom and specific to the donation, not a boilerplate message. When you use the same thank-you messaging for all donations, donors can sense that it's a form letter and you'll lose the impact of the thanks. Personalize the thank-you note to the original appeal so the donor will truly know the organization appreciated his gift. It would be best if you spent as much time crafting the thank-you note as you did the original appeal. I recommend writing the thank-you note at the same time as the appeal so you can match language and flow. This continuity lends to the impact of the messaging on the donor.

- **Give the donor credit**. This bit of advice will have a dramatic effect on the success of your donor communications if implemented throughout your donor-facing correspondence. The content of your thank-you letter and each piece you send out should position the donor as the hero in the story. This is likely the hardest thing for general nonprofit staff to grasp, as the people doing the work are often positioned as the hero, or the organization is positioned as the hero. However, in this case, the donor is the true hero of your organization. Without the donation, none of what you do would be possible. Even more importantly, positioning the donor as the hero will allow him/her to see the organization as the tool by which s/he can accomplish good. This is simpler than you think. Read your thank-you note and count how many times you use "we" or "I." Now count how many times you use "you" or "your." You should use "you" and "your" as the primary tool to communicate in the letter instead of "we" or "I." You want to position the communication from the donor's point of view, not from the organization. For example, instead of saying *We fed 1,100 families this Thanksgiving*, you could say, *Your donation, along with other donors like you, fed 1,100 families this Thanksgiving.* The difference involves the donor being included in the work. Giving the donor credit is a powerful way to strengthen the donor relationship.

- **Send a handwritten note**. Instead of a form letter or a thank-you email, send a handwritten note. In today's digital and cookie-cutter environment, personalizing and handwriting a note to the donor will demonstrate you care. This is a great activity for board members or volunteers. You should provide sample copy for what you want the thank-you note to say, keeping in mind the effective techniques of positioning the donor as the hero, sending it promptly, demonstrating impact, and making the donor feel truly appreciated.

- **Send a thank-you video**. Another creative way to say thank-you that will have a big impact on the donor is to send a custom thank-you video message. A custom video message is exactly that. Record a thank-you video for each person who donates. For larger organizations, this may be reserved for major, mid-level, or continuity donors. The script for the thank-you video doesn't have to be lengthy. Instead, it's important to acknowledge the donor by name in the first few seconds, acknowledge and thank them for their specific gift, and then explain what impact the donor will have. Demonstrate gratitude in your video and also tell the donor the next steps if there are any.

- **Make a phone call**. Demonstrate your gratitude by calling and thanking the donor. The phone is still a personal way of communicating and it helps build authenticity with the donor when s/he is called from a real person from your organization. The phone call provides a way to thank the donor and allow the donor to ask questions about the organization.

- **Create a photo book**. If you're raising money for a project or a specific campaign, take photos from inception to completion and create a photo book for the donor. A photo book that contains photos from the project can connect the donor to the work that s/he helped fund.

- **Send an anniversary card**. At the anniversary of a donor's first gift to your organization, send an anniversary card celebrating the donor and your year-long relationship. This is a way to demonstrate your gratitude for the donor's loyalty and that you're paying attention to the relationship. This is a key tool many organizations use to move donors to that second gift, if they were previously a "one-and-done" donor. You can have a member of the board, a volunteer, or the executive director sign the anniversary card.

- **Invite the donor to the office for a tour.** Invite the donor to tour your offices. This personal touch helps endear donors to your organization by introducing them to the real live people who are doing the day-to-day work the donor makes possible. Giving an office tour often results in connections you weren't expecting. For example, we've performed office tours that have resulted in corporate donor relationships, free press, and connections to influencers. These unexpected outcomes were a result of connecting the right person to the mission and having him/her provide an introduction that we would likely have never had. You never know what happens when you help a donor connect to the cause and meet people within your nonprofit.

- **Send a unique gift from your work.** If your work has artisan beneficiaries or you have a work program that produces products, create a custom thank-you gift for donors. When you send a thank-you gift to donors, you don't want it to be too elaborate as the donor may feel like you're spending the donation on the gift instead of the work. This type of gift takes many forms. It could be a basket, a unique wood carving, a picture frame, or a small keepsake.

- **Host a donor appreciation party**. Invite your donors to a donor appreciation party to recognize their support of your work. This is not an opportunity to ask for a donation, but simply a way to demonstrate gratitude for their continued partnership. What you'll find is that the donors will naturally feel like giving to your organization after attending a celebration like this. I recommend inviting a keynote speaker that will draw donors to your event. Alternatively, it can be as simple as an hors d'ouvres time that allows donors to meet and mingle with your staff. Another effective use of this type of party is to invite a beneficiary who has seen different aspects of your program and benefited from them. For example, if you have an organization that supports inner-city kids, invite a college graduate who experienced the program as a youth to tell his/her story of how the program benefited them and how s/he was able to graduate college because of your work.

- **Send a custom postcard**. Take a behind-the-scenes photo of your work and send it to the donor.

This spontaneous and unique way of displaying gratitude will demonstrate that you care about the relationship with the donor. There are several different apps — both for your phone and desktop — that you can use to print and mail a custom postcard. It usually costs between $1 and $2 for each postcard. You could send a variety of different photos to different donors, providing a unique connection. When the donor sees the work you're doing with a real photo taken by a real person, it demonstrates authenticity. Creating trust in the donor will help to continue deepening your relationship with them.

The key to building a relationship and getting to a second gift, or continuing to receive donations from a donor, is to create an experience where they genuinely believe that they're a part of your good work. The donor has a desire to help make an impact in a given area and she wants to know the donation will be used effectively and efficiently. The best way to continue to nurture this relationship is through a heartfelt thank-you.

APPRECIATING VOLUNTEERS

From its first year to second year of existence, the literary council Reading Renaissance saw its volunteer attrition rate grow from 5% to 20%. This means the organization had to replace 20% of its volunteers each year. The board understood the urgency of this problem but didn't understand the core problem.

After doing research, the board members discovered that they didn't have a sufficient volunteer recognition program. Volunteers were leaving because Reading Renaissance didn't thank them and they didn't feel appreciated.

The board held an emergency meeting to explore trends in appreciating volunteers and brainstorm simple, inexpensive ways to recognize all those who help. The board selected the best ideas and created a calendar of events to show appreciation to their volunteers. This ranged from handwritten notes of thanks to a barbecue party. The board also created a milestone chart for honoring volunteers, such as a small floral arrangement after completing 100 work hours and a luncheon for volunteers who complete a large project.

The board recognized the need for a formal and consistent show of appreciation for volunteers. After just six months of their new recognition system, attrition dropped back down to 5%.

A thankful nonprofit doesn't just focus on donors but also creates an appreciation system to recognize and thank volunteers.

A thankful organization attracts volunteers with the immediacy of feeling appreciated. Sarah Reece is a volunteer with Junior Achievement of Central Florida and appreciates how she feels after volunteering.

"I have always enjoyed working with children and volunteering is a way of life for me. Junior Achievement is just one organization that I volunteer for but one I get immediate rewards," Sarah explains. "The students always welcome me when I come and let me know they look forward to seeing me the next week. Each child is so unique, and they have much they want to share during the lessons. This is very rewarding!"

The immediate feeling of gratitude helps retain volunteers. When a volunteer sees the impact of their time, it encourages him/her to continue volunteering and to invite others to volunteer.

"Anyone who has never volunteered is missing out on some of the best experiences in life and especially working with children. Preparing for the lesson each week does not take that long and the time in the class is so rewarding," said Sarah.

TAKE ACTION

1) Download the Showing Donors Gratitude Playbook from http://magneticnonprofit/thankful.

2) Promptly thank donors for their gifts.

3) Develop creative ways to thank your volunteers.

4) Complete the Showing Donors Gratitude Playbook guide and execute at least two of the listed steps in the next 90 days.

Attribute Three: Tenured

In the 1940s, Esther Heller began a long family tradition of supporting National Jewish Health as a member of the New York City auxiliary. One of 1,500 chapters around the country supporting National Jewish Health, the group hosted events such as dinners, flea markets, and bingo games. The group supported the hospital's patient care and research.

Esther's son Joe moved to California and pursued a 35-year career in education. In 1996, he retired as chair of the Department of Psychology at California State University, Sacramento. His mom's lifelong involvement inspired Joe to support National Jewish Health after a relocation to Arizona.

"I have focused my personal and professional efforts on prevention," said Joe. "With genetic research, I hope that we can prevent diseases from occurring."

Joe's story is a shared experience with tens of thousands of other donors who continue generational giving to nonprofits and churches, following in their parents' footsteps.

In the *Heart of the Donor Study*, Russ Reid studied the influence of parents on today's adults. The study found that parents who modeled specific behaviors led to children who now engage in those behaviors. For example, 55% of adults whose parents frequently gave to a place of worship now support a place of worship, compared to 24% of those who rarely or never saw their parents give to a place of worship.

Similarly, 52% of today's adults who watched their parents frequently give to nonprofits are now active donors, compared to 26% of those who rarely or never saw their parents give.

Volunteerism follows a similar trend in the data. Forty-nine percent of adults who saw their parents frequently volunteer are now volunteers, compared to 20% who rarely or never saw this behavior modeled. The study found that these six parental behaviors are connected to how their children, now adults, behave:

- Gave money to a church or place of worship

- Gave money to a nonprofit other than a place of worship

- Discussed with children what nonprofits they support and why

- Attended church or a place of worship with their children

- Volunteered with organizations other than a place of worship

- Encouraged children to volunteer time with a nonprofit organization

Parents who model these types of behavior have an 80% chance of raising a child who turns out to be a donor, compared to a 25% chance for those who don't. Parental giving is a stronger predictive factor than ethnicity, education, household income, and age.

Parents who give raise children who give and many of those children support the same organizations their parents did. Tenure isn't just a descriptive term for how long your organization has been around, but instead, the attraction of a tenured organization is both the longevity and the familiarity of giving.

How do you encourage this behavior with your donors?

Create content that teaches parents how to cultivate a giving heart in their children. At Food for the Hungry, we have several ebooks on this topic. Visit http://www.fh.org/resources to see examples.

Develop giving campaigns that involve children. Four times each year, we mail an activity piece to child sponsors to interact with the child they support. For example, during the fall, we send a back-to-school piece that includes photos of the sponsored child with an activity. The donor can send a note to their sponsored child and receive a note back. Activities that involve children help parents teach generosity.

ORGANIZATION LONGEVITY

The longevity of a nonprofit is an essential consideration for a supporter. The potential donor or staff member researching your organization want to know your nonprofit has a future. Though the length of time your organization has been around isn't a guarantee it will be around in the future, the human mind uses that as an indicator.

The length of time your organization has been in existence is part of the tenured characteristic of a Magnetic Nonprofit. This part of the tenured characteristic is not something your organization can control; it is merely a fact.

In 2018, Tearfund UK celebrated its 50th year and created a microsite [12] called, "We Won't Stop." On this microsite, the organization created a timeline of significant events in its history. Tearfund UK uses its tenure as a part of the story, but the primary purpose of the microsite is to be forward-looking and motivate donors to become involved *today.*

Tenure isn't limited to how many years the organization has been in existence. Characteristics such as the depth of work you've performed, your volume and efficiency in fundraising, and the breadth of relationships and

---

[12] https://www.tearfund.org/en/wewontstop/our_journey/

partnerships you've developed all factor into how tenured your organization is.

You can't control when your organization was founded. The longevity of the organization does have an attraction for some donors. What you can do is tell the story of your organization to build a sense of stability with potential donors, staff, and volunteers.

TELLING YOUR STORY

Though your organization may be relatively young, tell the story of your founding and how it led to the organization you are today to reinforce a feeling of tenure. Jena Lee Nardella, the founder of Blood:Water Mission, starts her story like this:

When I was twenty-one, a vision for something extraordinary came to me. It came not as a gentle suggestion, but as an overpowering desire for change. It came from a convergence of a global health emergency, a collection of young musicians, and a personal need to live out a promise I had made to a homeless man twelve years before.

The vision included serving African villages where women and children walk several miles a day to find water to keep them alive. It included advocating for families whose immune systems were so weak from HIV that diseases in that water caused mothers to bury their babies and children

*to bury their parents. It included providing clean water for
one thousand of those African communities.*

Jena explained her passion for building wells in her book,
One Thousand Wells. Jena reinforces the brand and a feeling of
tenure for the organization, though it was founded in 2004
— a relatively short time ago.

One thousand wells!

That's a significant goal and creates a sense that the
organization has a solid foundation when it pursues a massive
vision.

Donor surveys consistently find that more than 75% of
respondents who give more than once to a nonprofit did so
because the nonprofit shared stories of impact and explained
to donors how their funds were used. According to the *2016
Burk Donor Survey* of over 28,000 donors in the United States
and Canada, 78% of donors research before giving. Your
nonprofit must tell stories of impact to draw in new
supporters and motivate existing donors to become repeat
donors.

MENTAL EFFECT OF STORIES

In a 2006 study in Spain published in the journal
NeuroImage, researchers asked participants to read words
aloud with strong odor associations, as well as neutral words,
while scanning their brains with a magnetic resonance

imaging (MRI) machine. The study showed that when participants read words such as perfume or coffee, the part of their brain that processes fragrant smells lit up. Other studies have also found that when participants read metaphors aloud that contained words associated with other senses, those portions of the brains also showed activity. For example, if you said, "I shook the man's leathery hands," the part of your brain associated with perceiving texture through touch became active. While saying, "he had strong hands," did not.

Researcher Uri Hasson found that when a woman began telling a story, the brains of the participants in the research project synchronize. When she had activity in her insula, an emotional brain region, the listeners did too. When her frontal cortex lit up, so did theirs. By merely telling a story, the woman could plant ideas, thoughts, and emotions into the listeners' brains.

Several research projects have found that telling a story opens the listener to feeling empathy when simply stating facts about a problem did not.

Your stories of impact will have a profound influence on your audience and change the level of attraction your organization has.

THOUGHT LEADERSHIP

Thought leadership is another aspect of tenure that your organization can highlight. Often, a nonprofit has incredibly smart people leading the organization and documenting the programmatic model. Creating content to demonstrate thought leadership will raise the tenure of your organization.

Thought leadership is tapping into your knowledge, experience, and passion to answer the most important questions your audience has. Forbes defines a thought leader as:

An individual or firm whose prospects, clients, referral sources, intermediaries, and even competitors recognize as one of the foremost authorities in selected areas of specialization, resulting in its being the go-to individual or organization for said expertise.[13]

Embracing the role of a thought leader in your part of the nonprofit industry leads to more donors, favorable legislation, increased attractiveness for partners and new hires, and increased respect for your organization's work.

How do I develop a reputation as a thought leader?

---

[13] https://www.forbes.com/sites/russprince/2012/03/16/what-is-a-thought-leader/#c1592217da04

Identify the big questions being asked for the cause your organization works in and develop the right type of content to answer those questions. The content may be blog posts, articles, guest columns, videos, webinars, training courses, earned/paid media, or live speeches. Consistently producing the right answers will lead to recognition as a thought leader.

Thought leadership also attracts volunteers.

Nancy Wilson began volunteering with the Center for Internet Security because of the quality of the organization's work. She explains, "The best thing is the consensus development of recommendations which draws on the experience and expertise of the world-wide technology community. The CIS Benchmarks give technologists a place to start when evaluating the security needed for their systems. The guidance provided can be especially helpful for those who are not experts in a technology, for example, the 'accidental' Database Administrator."

The Center for Internet Security helps companies, governments, and organizations develop better data security practices. Paul Campbell, another volunteer for the organization, describes why the organization is so valued in the data security community. "They contain practical security recommendations. The content comes from a diverse set of contributors and considers realistic threats. The CIS Benchmarks content is then presented as a series of recommendations, with rationales, that should be considered by the implementer and selected as appropriate to their use case. People need to think for themselves when implementing controls and the CIS Benchmarks processes and philosophy support that." The thought leadership draws in volunteers like Nancy and Paul.

PARTNERSHIPS

A key way to attract supporters who appreciate tenure is through your partnerships. A nonprofit that is trusted by grant-making organizations, other non-governmental organizations (NGOs) and relief and development agencies builds magnetism in donors who are attracted to tenure.

If your organization receives grants for your work, tell that story to your donors. Grants are an indicator that the organization is vetted by other organizations.

Apply for government, corporate, and foundation grants to help develop this magnetic attribute.

Partnerships with other charities also demonstrate trustworthiness to donors. It provides a sense of tenure to the donors to know another charity has put their faith in the organization.

STABILITY

Donors are attracted to nonprofits they believe are stable. A sustainable nonprofit can survive an economic crisis, a dip in income, or the loss of a critical funder or program. The attributes of a tenured organization will help it survive. These include:

First, the programs need to have a genuine impact on the beneficiaries. If your cause is to end homelessness in the Columbus, Ohio, metropolitan area, but each year beneficiaries continue to remain in shelters, your programmatic model needs to change. You may be providing temporary housing, but you're not ending homelessness. Donors are attracted to a tenured nonprofit that accomplishes goals and makes a real impact with the people it serves.

Second, you need to develop a forward-looking financial vision and strategy. Many nonprofits close their doors because of poor cash flow planning and little to no cash reserves. Develop a multi-year plan and begin building cash reserves to survive unexpected events.

Third, you need a flexible programmatic model. Using the earlier example of a Columbus-based homeless ministry, if your model addresses apartment placement services for homeless men but doesn't address job placement, you may not be successful in solving the core problem. If someone can't maintain employment, he won't be able to afford the apartment on a long-term basis. Develop a comprehensive and relevant programmatic model to address each of the issues contributing to the problem you're solving.

TAKE ACTION

1. Write your founding story.

2. Download the hero's story framework from http://magneticnonprofit/tenured

3. Identify the key experts who you're going to ask to support your organization.

4. Research the five biggest questions your audience has and develop content to answer them.

Attribute Four: Timely

"We're at least two days out from having a story and we can't send the appeal until we have that story," my coworker explained to me. "Once we have that story, we can write the appeal and send it through approvals, so that may take another day."

I couldn't believe we were five days out from sending an emergency fundraising email! Though we were already sending supplies and people to the area, I was handcuffed from being able to send out an appeal at the peak of media attention.

Up until a few years ago, when a disaster struck, it would often take five or more days for Food for the Hungry to decide to respond and send out an email appeal. A direct mail appeal would take even longer, sometimes appearing in donor mailboxes four weeks or more after the disaster occurred.

The lack of timeliness not only made our fundraising suffer and produce unsatisfactory results, but it also contributed to a negative donor mindset — we were slow to respond. Donors didn't understand why our relief and humanitarian team were on the ground as quickly as possible, while our fundraising was so delayed.

We also compared poorly against other nonprofit organizations. Many of them had fundraising emails sent within a day or two of a disaster. If a donor who wants to respond to a disaster receives multiple emails from organizations they support financially, the donor wants his/her donation to have the quickest impact, so s/he will often give to the organization who sends the first email.

Our delays had to end. Unfortunately, this wasn't the only area where our timeliness was an issue.

Thank-you mailings were equally as slow. We didn't send out a proper thank-you email in a timely fashion, and the mailed receipt would often be more than a week out. The receipt the donor did receive was generic and had no unique message of thanks based on what their financial gift supported. System limitations prevented us from genuinely personalizing emails and mailed receipts, resulting in a generic form letter-feel for both.

Outside of child sponsors, we didn't have a welcome packet or email welcome series. We were struggling by not correctly on-boarding new donors. In short, we were failing at promptly communicating.

Donors are attracted to an organization based on how timely they are.

At Food for the Hungry, we learned that donors thought our communications were slow, and at times, there were questions about whether or not we were responsive. It wasn't easy, but we needed to address this problem and make timeliness a priority.

We addressed the timeliness of sending out disaster appeals by reducing the number of people who need to approve a response and by preparing pre-written templates for different types of disasters. These can be quickly customized when a disaster strikes. We created a new structure for disasters so the project team can quickly focus their efforts on the response. We cut average email send time down from 3 days to 4 hours.

We also created a process to provide a file of emergency donors to our vendors each month and prepositioned templates at the print vendor. Now, when a disaster strikes and we decide to raise funds through direct mail, we've cut production time down to just a few days.

We also discovered that we weren't responsive sending receipts and thank-you letters. We changed the system to allow personalized receipting based on how much was donated, and we customized our email receipt. These changes have produced better quality communications that are more meaningful to our donors.

The timely nonprofit is one where the communications align with a donor's expectations. The timely nonprofit sends appeals soon after events that facilitate a need, sends thank-you notes within a day of receiving a donation, and sends communications to volunteers to keep them engaged. The timely nonprofit understands the cadence of communicating with supporters and doesn't over-send or under-send.

It's time for you to assess how timely your nonprofit organization communicates with its donors.

DONOR COMMUNICATIONS

In the study described in Chapter 1 to determine how 167 nonprofits responded to the question, "*My husband and I are looking to donate to a nonprofit like yours. Why should we donate to your organization versus another organization, or not at all?*", nearly 40% of the organizations took a week to respond and 43% took over a month to respond — or worse, didn't respond at all.

Do you spend time debating your content marketing strategy or social media plan, but then miss the essential communications to donors?

You're not alone.

We don't honor our supporters when we miss the small opportune moments of human connection.

Follow these three steps to improve donor communication:

First, create multiple opportunities for people to connect. As I tested nonprofits, I found many instances where the nonprofit didn't have a contact form on their website, or they had turned off the ability to send a Facebook message. In these instances, they've blocked the ability to connect with donors using their preferred method of communication.

As we increasingly move to a personalized media environment, forcing your supporter to use only one channel of communication will cause you to lose support. Millennials don't want to call or email you. Generation X would prefer to send a quick email or use a website chat option. An older generation may prefer to call and speak to a real person.

There are constraints. You may not have the resources to provide all of these communication channels. In these instances, use technology to help you. There are inexpensive tools to manage digital communications, such as a tool to create a bot that can help manage Facebook Messenger (like ManyChat).

Being flexible in how a donor can communicate with you helps your organization become more magnetic.

Second, be responsive. Many times, connecting via a digital channel can feel a little like your message is going into a black hole. If someone sends a direct social media message or email, make sure to respond as quickly as possible, even if you need to research the issue. Email acknowledgment breeds good feelings in your supporter.

The first step in being a timely communicator is to respond in a reasonable timeframe. How you respond to donors (and how quickly you do it) is crucial when building good relationships. Use the email recipient's first name. If possible, have a staff member (as opposed to a generic title or your organization name) respond, so the recipient connects a real person to your nonprofit organization. For example, don't sign off an email with "Sincerely yours, Donor Service Representative." Send the email from a real person. People want to interact with other people.

Third, provide an answer to the question the person is asking. Many times, in the study, I found the responses were lacking in information. The nonprofit didn't answer the question and instead, pointed me to the website. A timely nonprofit responds in an appropriate amount of time and also responds with a detailed answer to the question asked. Read how one nonprofit answered the question:

Hi Jessica,

Thank you for reaching out, you can find out where your donations would go by visiting this link: https://www.organization.org/save-now/where-your-money-goes

Thanks-
Organization Name

Unfortunately, this doesn't answer *why* Jessica should choose to donate to this organization versus any other. This particular organization is huge, so it likely isn't a resource or staff size problem that prohibits them from taking a few minutes and craft a concise and informative response.

Train your staff to answer the question asked. It can be frustrating for a donor to keep sending more communications to have a simple question answered.

SHOWING GRATITUDE

Delaying your initial thank-you note, letter, or email after a donation comes in by as little as a few days can have a detrimental impact on repeat gifts from donors. About a third of donors said they would consider a second gift if they received a thank-you note from a nonprofit, yet only 61% reported receiving such a note after donating! [14]

This number doesn't surprise me as my anecdotal evidence suggests it's accurate. I give donations to a variety of organizations to see how their process works and to find out what types of communications I'll receive as a donor. It surprises me how few organizations thank me — even digitally, the lowest cost form of gratitude. When I do receive a thank-you card, it warms my heart. With few organizations doing it, it is an easy way to set your organization apart from others.

Your donor gratitude communications should be sent no later than 48 hours after a donation. For digital donations, I recommend you send digital demonstrations of gratitude

---

[14] https://www.cygresearch.com/files/free/2017_Burk_Donor_Survey_Report _US_Executive_Summary.pdf

immediately. We explore donor gratitude more deeply in the Thankful Magnetic Nonprofit attribute section.

EMERGENCY COMMUNICATIONS

How do you speed up response to events and donors?

First, you need intelligent monitoring processes and tools. When something external occurs, such as a disaster, you need to be aware of it as quickly as possible. This will likely be a combination of systems and people. A system is a process to identify an external event run by people. The combination allows you to make intelligent decisions quickly.

Second, your nonprofit needs a well-conceived process to respond in case of an emergency. Develop a written plan for what steps your team should follow during a disaster. Include checklists, staff assignments, and appeal templates.

At Food for the Hungry, we've developed a Crisis Management Team process that is initiated by the CEO in case there is a crisis that exists outside of our staff's ability to manage within our existing structure. For example, if a staff member is kidnapped, the CEO would initiate a Crisis Management Team. A situation of this magnitude requires a timely response from your nonprofit.

Third, you need to identify a plan to respond to a PR crisis or event that impacts your staff, leadership,

or organization. Developing the plan ahead of time is essential. When you're in the middle of a crisis, you don't need the added stress of trying to figure out all of the steps you should take. Missing a step could be detrimental to your organization.

During the Ebola outbreak of 2014, the American Association of Critical-Care Nurses (AACN) followed a disaster response protocol to assess situations and plan responses to crises that affected the critical care nursing community.

AACN then released training and webinars, teaching the implications of caring for patients with serious diseases such as Ebola Virus Disease (EVD). It brought together experts and nurses from Emory University Hospital who had first-hand experience caring for patients with EVD.

The organization became a popular source for experts on EVD. As the public's attention grew, the media turned to AACN for stories.

Developing a crisis communications plan helped the AACN get ahead of the EVD crisis and respond both to the needs of its members and the public.

Fourth, your organization needs to improve the timeliness of communications to your donors. These steps require you to perform a communications audit to understand what is being communicated and when it's being communicated.

A communications audit is simple to do. Create a list of standard communications and when the recipient would receive the communication on the journey with you. In the case of an emergency, document what types of communication you would expect the recipient to receive. I've developed a free communications audit template for you that you can download at http://magneticnonprofit.com/timely.

Fifth, create a supporter journey for each audience segment to understand what is being communicated. Now that you've audited which communications your audience is currently receiving, it's time to decide what they should be receiving. Create a supporter journey that shows the planned communications for different types of supporters.

Our first supporter journey was created using post-it notes and later translated into a digital version. We identified supporters such as a new lead, general donor, child sponsor, mid-level donor, major donor, and volunteer.

For each supporter, we documented a specific journey.

Developing these communication plans creates a feeling with your supporter that your organization is timely.

COMMUNICATING WITH VOLUNTEERS

In 1891, Salvation Army Captain Joseph McFee set up the first red kettle at the Oakland Ferry Landing near San Francisco. He used the grassroots fundraiser to host a holiday meal for the hungry in this area. The idea quickly spread. In 2016, the Red Kettle Campaign brought in $147 million with more than 25,000 volunteers. The Salvation Army needs a well-oiled machine to recruit and manage that many volunteers.

Local chapters of the Salvation Army start their holiday volunteer planning in August with a postcard campaign to bell ringers from previous years. At the same time, they begin using social media ads and direct mail to find new volunteers. Their messaging connects the bell-ringing hours directly to the impact on programs and services. For example, four hours of bell-ringing will feed a family for a week.

From the moment someone signs up to be a bell ringer to the time they volunteer, the Salvation Army communicates promptly so they don't lose the volunteer. Twenty-four to 72 hours before their scheduled time, the Salvation Army sends volunteers an email and/or a phone call to confirm their shift. Each volunteer is thanked after their service and also mailed a post-Christmas impact report showing the value of their service.

The process is very dependent on proper planning and timing in order to have a successful bell ringing season of giving. The lesson we learn from the Salvation Army is to be timely in our campaigns, from finding volunteers to thanking them and reporting on the impact they made.

A decision to support your organization is at the intersection of your offer and the right timing for the supporter. This is true whether it's a donation, volunteer request, or even a job offer. Create more opportunities for connection by becoming a timely nonprofit.

TAKE ACTION

1) Go to http://magneticnonprofit.com/timely for templates and a communications plan.

2) Perform a communications audit. An example is included at the link above.

3) Create a communications calendar.

4) Increase the frequency of communications to staff and volunteers. Be more transparent about the state of your organization.

5) Measure your response time for communications and set small goals to improve. Each time you achieve your new response time, set a new goal. Over time, your communications will become timelier.

Attribute Five: Testimony

Andreas Albert Nord, known to friends and family as Andy, developed a crippling form of arthritis early in life. Andy believed research was vital in preventing the disease and the life-altering effects. He left a gift to the University of British Columbia to benefit rheumatology research.

"My hope is to find better ways to live with the disease, and to find the cause, leading to a cure once and for all," Andy said. He had 13 major surgeries for cancer and arthritis. Between the two, Andy believed arthritis had a more devastating impact on his life. Andy's gift is an example of his commitment to end something that had a significant effect on his life by donating to an organization fighting for his cause.

Like Andy, many of us support organizations that are fighting for a cause we have a personal affinity for. In Andy's case, the gift to the University of British Columbia was to help find a cure for debilitating arthritis, something he personally suffered with. For others, it may be a gift to a cancer organization because their mom had cancer, or a gift to a hospital because of the excellent treatment received, or volunteering at a child's school. In all of these cases, testimony attracted people to support a specific cause.

Each of us has a story. In our story there are life events that dramatically impact who we are. These life events may even change the life of a loved one. Whatever they may be, an adverse life event leaves a lasting emotional impact and a desire to make a difference so others don't have the same experience. If the event was positive, we give so others can experience a positive impact.

The testimony is the part of you that is impacted by life's events. A Magnetic Nonprofit speaks to someone's testimony.

A supporter will resonate with your testimony magnetism in two ways: a direct connection and one on the periphery of life.

DIRECT TESTIMONY

A direct testimony is when a supporter feels a personal connection to a cause because of something that has impacted his life, good or bad. When you are communicating with someone who has a direct link to your cause, you will often create a passionate response. The emotional response from being directly affected is stronger than having a connection to someone directly impacted.

The direct testimony could be something that impacted another person but had a strong influence on the supporter's life. For example, a man whose mother died of cancer may have a direct testimony because of the negative emotions the cancer caused him to experience with his mother's passing. Though he doesn't have cancer, he may feel strong emotions and desire to donate to cancer-fighting organizations.

PERIPHERY TESTIMONY

Periphery testimony occurs when friends, coworkers, community members, or even acquaintances of an individual are impacted by something that happens in the individual's life. For example, you may have a neighborhood friend whose husband has heart disease. When the family raises money for a heart disease foundation, you give because of a periphery testimony. Generally, the periphery testimony has a weaker response from a supporter compared to the direct testimony.

Life events and things that impact people can be positive or negative. For example, a young lady who had a positive experience growing up with a tutor that changed her education would probably passionately support a tutoring nonprofit. This positive experience impacted her life and she wants to share the experience with others who need tutoring. Likewise, if someone had diabetes and donates to an organization searching for a cure, s/he is reacting to a negative life experience by trying to help other people not suffer. Neither type of motivation is good or bad, nor is either one more impactful than the other. In the first example, the donor may be just as passionate about tutoring as a person with diabetes is passionate about ending suffering in the second example. Your organization's attractiveness for testimony depends on your areas of focus.

You can appeal to someone who is driven by a personal testimony by sharing success stories. When you share stories that a donor can relate to, s/he is more likely to give to your organization.

HOW DO YOU ATTRACT PEOPLE WITH TESTIMONY?

Testimony requires an organization to be a good storyteller. Storytelling organizations can reach supporters who have a testimony connection to the cause. Simply stating you're working to end diabetes isn't enough. The organization should show excellent work through stories of beneficiaries, research, and successful results.

Stories from a nonprofit should cast a big vision for the reader. You are making a significant impact for beneficiaries and you want the reader to understand that. A good story structure is universal: you have the hero, also known as the protagonist; you have a guide helping the hero; you have a villain, such as hunger, poverty, or cancer; and you have a journey. The hero of the story is the donor: How do you place the reader into the story so they can see themself helping the cause? When you're able to position the reader as the hero and your organization as the guide helping the hero, you are more likely to turn the reader into a donor.

The best nonprofit story is the "story of the one." The story of the one focuses on a single beneficiary and tells the story of his/her life before s/he received help, a description of how the organization helped, and what his/her life is like now that s/he has received support. Focusing on how the donor helped the beneficiary move through this process is critical for the reader to believe s/he can make a difference in the beneficiary's life.

Transforming your organization into a storytelling organization is a process. **First, you need to get senior leadership buy-in** to teach storytelling techniques to all staff members. The best way to accomplish this is to demonstrate the difference between organizations that do and don't use storytelling in their fundraising. There is much research on the topic of how donors want to see how their donation is being used and understand the impact the organization is having. When the entire organization is part of the story-gathering process and understands the positive impact stories have, staff will feel both empowered and excited to participate.

New Story, a nonprofit using 3D printing to build houses, understood the power of stories when they launched three years ago. The founding leadership team leveraged the press and stories of struggles by other nonprofits in Haiti. In four years, they've built 1,600 homes, and in 2017, they raised $5.6 million, up from $3.8 million in 2016.

Host a storytelling workshop for staff members to learn how to identify, collect, and tell good stories. Use examples of well-written and poorly-written stories, and how staff members can have a positive impact on the organization's growth. Give your staff a hands-on opportunity during these workshops to practice story gathering and storytelling.

Create a template to help your staff gather stories. The template should include open-ended questions and the specific details they'll need to gather to tell a good story. Provide a mechanism for staff members to submit their stories. Follow up during meetings, monthly newsletters, and the company intranet to keep storytelling top of mind for your staff.

Create an editorial schedule of the type of stories needed. Share it with your staff so they can watch out for relevant stories during the course of their daily work that fit your needs. After you use a story, share the engagement results with the story gatherers. Sharing results will help your staff feel motivated that the stories they gather have a direct impact on the organization.

TESTIMONY DRIVES DONATIONS

As a journalist for almost 50 years, Phil Currie discovered that the principles of writing compelling, credible, and relevant pieces are what guided his career. He started as an editor at the University of Iowa's student newspaper and made it all the way to the senior vice president of news for Gannet Co., Inc, the largest newspaper group in America. Phil understands what it takes to write a story that inspires readers.

It was this gift of inspiration that drove him to become a legacy donor at Newseum, the museum commemorating free press in Washington, D.C.

"Because I have been a journalist all my life, I find the Newseum [museum] significant and moving, reinforcing almost 50 years in the field for me," Phil said. "At the Newseum, you get a sense of the role journalism has played in our history. It isn't just about our profession. It's about history; the way things were reported. The back and forth of journalists had an impact on what happened."

Today, Phil is among the first members of the Newseum's Legacy Society, which acknowledges the generosity of those who have chosen to remember the museum in their wills, or through another type of bequest.

"For me, this is one last 'thank you' for all that has been done through the First Amendment," he said. "An understanding that a free press has been a huge part of history and understanding what's happening in our democracy is important.

"The Newseum can be one of the strongest institutions we have to convey the importance of democracy and freedom of press. If people are looking for a place for lasting support and impact, the Newseum is the place."

Phil's long career in journalism inspired his giving to an institution that shares similar values. This is the power of testimony: people want to support something that has an impact on their lives.

Don't forget to tell the testimony stories of donors who give to your organization. Donors want to see people just like them giving to your organization and hear a testimony of why they gave. Compelling testimonies are a powerful tool for attracting new donors.

TESTIMONY ATTRACTS EMPLOYEES & VOLUNTEERS

Like Phil, Jeannie Montano has a passion for the work of the nonprofits she's joined.

"My mother has always been my biggest advocate, from the time she raised me in the Bronx to encouraging me to follow my passion and work at impactful community organizations," said Jeannie Montano, CEO of United Way of the Dutchess-Orange Region, explaining how she came to work in the nonprofit sector.

Jeannie suffered the tragic loss of her young brother to blood cancer. After a career in airline management and publishing, Jeannie found her true calling beginning at The Leukemia & Lymphoma Society.

For many employees, it is crucial to have a shared testimony with the mission of the organization. For Jeannie, joining the United Way was an extension of who she already was. Jeannie explains, "I love to be part of an organization that truly helps the community."

When you're looking for staff, hire for passion as much as for knowledge and expertise. When an employee at a nonprofit aligns with the mission and vision for the organization, s/he will handle the cycles of working at a nonprofit better than if s/he is just there for a job.

A Magnetic Nonprofit creates an environment where it empowers hiring managers to select the best staff who have a heart for accomplishing the vision of the organization.

Testimony often attracts volunteers. Andres Esteller began volunteering at the Humane Society of North Central Florida to help his wellbeing.

"Last year I had the realization that I was spending too much time worrying about things outside of my control, and it was doing some harm to my emotional health," Andres explains. "That is why I decided I would ask myself what was within my power to change, and the animal shelter was the first thought I had. I have always been passionate about caring and looking after our furry friends, they understand us in ways people can't, and in helping them I believe I am doing a great service to my community, as my actions contribute towards the nurturing of animals that will be adopted by countless people who will give them the love they so greatly deserve."

Like Andres, Allie Huffstutler felt a deep connection to the National Blood Clot Alliance and began volunteering. Allie remembers the day her radiologist gave her urgent news,

"You have blood clots throughout your body and in your lungs. I'm not sure how you are alive right now."

Allie had trouble breathing for two weeks and sought medical help for what she believed was a pulled muscle. She first visited a quick-care clinic, but then was swiftly sent to the emergency room where she received the diagnosis. As a part of healing from this traumatic experience, Allie supports the National Blood Clot Alliance to help other people in a similar situation.

A SUPPORTER'S INNER CIRCLE

Many times, an individual's life is impacted by friends and family experiencing life events. Close relationships deepened John and Betty Fitzpatrick's connection to Mercy Medical Center.

"So many of our friends are having strokes and heart problems," Betty said. "If we can take care of them sooner and better, it will limit the damage done (to their heart or brain). We can afford to support that. It's important to us."

John and Betty are longtime supporters of the Mercy Hospice, Pediatric Care at Mercy Redding, and Mercy's Emergency Department Renovation and Expansion.

"It's important to have high-quality care here," Betty said. "As you grow older, you appreciate being taken care of in your own community."

John and Betty donated to Mercy Medical Center at different stages of their life when various health conditions impacted friends and family. Lives around them drive their testimony.

As a nonprofit, you're not only trying to reach an audience that has an affinity for your cause because they were directly impacted, but you should also be speaking to an audience who has had their lives affected by testimonies from other people.

Involving your staff in storytelling is one of the steps required for you to become a leader that honors testimony.

Testimony is a strong motivator for donors, staff, and volunteers. Don't forget to include the latter two groups with stories that have a direct impact on them. For staff, you can share stories in internal newsletters and the company intranet that speak to their connection to the causes of the organization. When you're recruiting, updating, and thanking volunteers, make sure to include stories that speak to testimony.

TAKE ACTION

1. Download the story gathering framework from http://magneticnonprofit/testimony, to create a library of supporters, staff, and beneficiary testimonies.

2. Hold a workshop for internal staff to understand story-gathering techniques for testimonies.

3. Create an easy way (such as an email address) for supporters, staff, and beneficiaries to submit testimonies.

4. Create an editorial schedule to share testimonies in social media, newsletters, and your organization's website.

Attribute Six: Tribe

While walking on a street in India, Adam Braun asked a boy who was on the street begging, "What do you want most in the world?"

The boy replied, "a pencil."

Adam reached into his backpack, pulled out a pencil, and gave it to this boy. He watched as the boy's face lit up as he realized what he could do with this simple gift. At that moment, Adam committed to helping as many kids as he could.

As Adam explained it, "That answer changed my life."

Adam backpacked across 50 countries, handing out pens and pencils to children, giving them hope one child at a time. Adam began a career in finance but believed he could approach the nonprofit sector with a different point of view. "I'd seen so many ineffective organizations that I became obsessed with bringing top-notch business acumen into the humanitarian sector."

In October, 2008, Adam walked into a local bank and deposited $25 in hopes of building one school in a developing country by asking people to give up their birthdays and ask their family and friends to donate instead. Pencils of Promise was born.

2008 was a difficult time to start a nonprofit. From 2008 to 2012, 12,831 nonprofits[15] who reported more than $50,000 in income shut down. Adam didn't have major donors backing Pencils of Promise, so he had to be strategic with fundraising in an economic downturn.

If Adam made the wrong bet, he'd be one of the almost 13,000 nonprofits that shut down from 2008 to 2012. Adam made two bets:

First, the organization bet that social media would become the fabric of society. Second, they bet on the rise of cause marketing.

He built a digital community that went on to become the lifeblood of Pencils of Promise and have started over 35,000 personal fundraisers for the organization.

In 2008, Adam turned that $25 into $58,772 in contributions. The next year, $84,865. He started to see some payoff from his efforts in building a community.

The following year, Pencils of Promise exploded to $1.45 million in revenue. Like all fundraising, building a tribe takes time, but when done right, it can result in massive growth for your organization.

---

[15] https://www.urban.org/sites/default/files/publication/24046/412924-The-Impact-of-the-Great-Recession-on-the-Number-of-Charities.PDF

In 2017, Pencils of Promise grew to $11,125,626. The organization broke ground on their 400th school and have 90,000 active students.

Pencils of Promise learned a nonprofit is magnetic when it becomes a part of the donor's tribe.

BECOME A PART OF YOUR DONOR'S TRIBE

Let me emphasize this point: your organization is becoming a part of the *donor's* tribe.

When you put your nonprofit at the center of the tribe, you've failed. The tribe is about the common thread that runs through its members, it is not about your organization.

Pencils of Promise made an early bet at the time social media was starting to gain traction. Your organization has an opportunity to become a part of your donor's tribe.

Adam Braun explains, "Social networks don't get people to donate, they get people to connect to your mission. And once they're connected to your mission, they'll not only donate, their peers will donate to you too because they'll see how important your work is to their friend."

SOCIAL IDENTITY

In the 1970s, a psychologist named Henri Tafjel developed a theory called "social identity."[16] Social identity suggests that as we define ourselves, we do so in large part by asserting loyalty to the groups we are a part of. Tafjel developed the theory after performing research that shows humans are quick to organize themselves into groups and when they do, they immediately form a negative about and act against competing groups.

The interesting thing about Tafjel's studies is that the formation of the group can be about something completely meaningless. In one study, people were shown 40 dots for half a second. They were asked to estimate how many dots they saw. The number was meaningless, Tafjel flipped to a coin to label someone as an over estimator or an under estimator. Once the subject was told which he was, he was asked to help with another experiment.

The participant was told there was a certain amount of money that would be split between over estimators and under estimators in a separate study. The participant himself wasn't going to receive any money. Even though the only thing connecting the study participant with the groups was the label of over estimator or under estimator, subjects tended to

---

16 https://youarenotsosmart.com/transcripts/transcript-tribal-psychology/

split the money in favor of their group every time. Study participants favored one group over the other solely based on a label randomly assigned by Tafjel.

Tafjel repeated the study multiple times in different ways. In one study, he showed two abstract art paintings labeled Artist A and Artist B and people were told they were in a group that liked Artist A or a different group that preferred Artist B, when the subject joined the group, he showed favoritism to members of his group. In a different study, people were randomly labeled as a part of a group number, like Group 40, and then demonstrated favoritism to members of their group and negative actions to members of other groups.

Humans instinctively form groups that in turn lead to actively supporting the group they are in and competing against the ones they are not in.

A DONOR'S TRIBE

Donors support organizations that close friends and family support. Seth Godin made the word "tribe" famous in business circles in his book *Tribes: We Need You to Lead Us* where he defines it as any group of people, large or small, which are connected to one another, a leader, or an idea. In the Magnetic Nonprofit, a tribe can be a strong attraction for donors, employees, and volunteers.

Unfortunately, many nonprofits fail to understand how donors want to interact. A mistaken view of a tribe is to imagine the hub and spoke model:

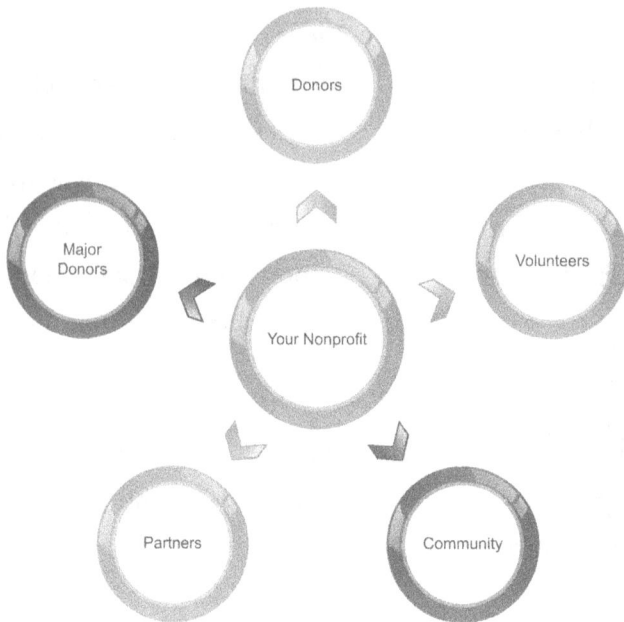

Magnetic Nonprofits don't build a tribe with the organization at the center. Instead, the nonprofit is a part of the donor's tribe. The nonprofit is simply a member, not the driving force in a tribe. When you begin seeing the organization as a member of a tribe, you begin to understand the amount of value you need to bring people to be an influential member of the tribe.

How does your nonprofit become a part of the donor's tribe?

Your nonprofit should identify the tribes to become a part of, provide value to the community, tell stories of impact, and be clear with what you're asking for.

First, you should identify tribes that you can participate in. There are a variety of ways that someone is attracted to a nonprofit due to involvement with a tribe. Someone could come to support a nonprofit:

At an event. Someone could experience a nonprofit appeal at an event. For example, many Christian nonprofits raise funds by appealing for donors at concerts. The audience member came for one purpose, a concert, but was so motivated by the tribe (led by the music artist) that she gave to the nonprofit.

At a fundraising event. A potential donor could be invited to a fundraising event and influential friends help push him/her to give. Inviting people who are all part of the same tribe is a common tactic for major donor fundraising. Influencers in the tribe help motivate giving.

Through influencers. Influencers can motivate people in a tribe to give to a particular nonprofit. Earlier, I shared how I became a donor of Pencils of Promise because of a podcast host I listen to. I am in the audience of this niche and the podcast host has talked a couple of times about his support of Pencils of Promise. The podcast host is moved by the organization's work and starts sharing with his audience. Many nonprofits cultivate an influencer program to create opportunities just like this.

From a celebrity. Celebrities and other influencers hold tremendous sway over people in their tribe. When a celebrity selects a cause to support, he or she can move many people in the tribe to support that organization. The Ice Bucket Challenge for ALS is a great example of a viral campaign that became so popular because of celebrity involvement.

At the workplace. The United Way and many community foundations run successful fundraising campaigns through workplace giving. The tribe of the workplace is a motivator to support an organization your employee chooses.

WHAT TYPES OF TRIBES WILL YOU GET INVOLVED IN?

Create a list of potential tribes your organization can participate in. The list should include social media groups and hashtags, influencers, common interest groups, corporations, events you sponsor, local community groups, religious groups, and other potential tribes you can become involved in.

Second, your nonprofit should provide value to the community. When a tribe forms around a given topic or purpose, the members that provide value are known and trusted. For example, if your nonprofit wants to become a member of a tribe at a workplace and participate in workplace giving in a meaningful way, your organization should provide the people at the company who are responsible for workplace giving campaigns easy-to-use materials promoting ways employees can give. Your organization should also provide tools and stories for employees to know where their money is going and the impact it will have.

Another common community is one that forms around a specific cause your nonprofit is working towards. For example, there are people in your town who are passionate about helping at-risk youth. If your organization wants to connect with these people, provide tools they can use to volunteer or to participate in the lives of at-risk youth to make a difference. Providing value to the community, while asking for nothing in return, helps members of the tribe to know and trust your nonprofit.

At Food for the Hungry, we have several professional athletes who want to encourage their fanbase to support the work we do. We found that by providing easy to use tools and stories, photos, and videos, it takes the pressure off the athlete to try and create his own. He can quickly tell the story of FH to his audience and get them to become passionate about a cause he's passionate for.

Coty Sensabaugh, cornerback for the Pittsburgh Steelers, has a passion for helping provide clean water to kids in Haiti.

"Just seeing how much the kids in the area had to go through to get clean water — a lot of kids in the area couldn't even go to school on a regular basis because they had to go fetch water for their families,[17]" Sensabaugh said. "I'm not talking about five or 10 minutes — they had to walk four or five hours per day just to get clean water for their families. So once we saw it with our own eyes, it was a no brainer for us."

One of the campaigns Sensabaugh participated in provided an opportunity for a donor and a guest to attend a football game as a guest of Sensabaugh. Food for the Hungry provided all of the messaging, the platform for the campaign, and sent someone to the game to help the winners and Sensabaugh. Providing the support to someone as busy as Sensabaugh makes it easy for him to give back by activating his tribe to support the cause of clean water.

Third, your nonprofit should tell stories of impact. Stories of impact demonstrate the good work you do and the problem you solve. Telling stories of impact builds trust with your tribe that you do what you say you do with

---

[17] http://post-gazette.com/sports/steelers/2017/11/14/coty-sensabaugh-steelers-haiti-food-for-the-hungry/stories/201711040020

their donation. Unfortunately, many nonprofits struggle with telling an effective story and are left with dull "impact reports" that are full of statistics, but not life-changing stories.

Maya Angelou said it best, "People will forget what you said, people will forget what you did, but they will never forget how you made them feel."

Why tell stories of impact?

Using a story helps the reader put themselves in the place of being able to help that specific beneficiary. The story fires in parts of the brain where the reader can experience the emotions in the story. When you tell a story of transformation, the reader can feel how the beneficiary feels having his life changed.

We have a long tradition of storytelling. For many people, telling stories is the ideal way for them to learn. Telling a story helps someone connect with a storyteller uniquely. Several studies have shown that the brain stimulation that occurs during storytelling has a unique way of syncing to the same areas of the brain firing between a storyteller and someone hearing the story. In other words, the reader or listener can feel and think the same as the storyteller. If you tell a compassionate story that moves someone to get involved, you can transmit the thoughts of the storyteller to the story listener. Storytelling is a powerful way to move someone to become involved with your nonprofit.

WRITING A GOOD STORY THAT ATTRACTS MEMBERS OF A TRIBE

Stories attract members of a tribe to your organization when people hear a story they can relate to. There are 6 key elements to writing a good story:

1. **The Relatable Central Character:** The beneficiary is the central character in the story. He faces a challenge that he cannot overcome on his own, so he needs help in the form of the hero (the donor) and the organization. The relatable central character needs a story arc of going through a transformation and overcoming something. This transformation cannot occur without help from the donor and nonprofit organization. The story should be about a real person. If you can't use real names for privacy purposes, use a pseudonym, just make sure you use a name to connect the reader to the central character.

2. **The Hero:** The donor is the hero of the story. This point is often difficult to overcome for folks inside a nonprofit as they want to see the nonprofit or their own staff as the hero. But in the end, in order for an appeal to work right, your organization is not the hero, the donor is. You see, without the donor, the transformation can never happen. The reader needs to put themselves in the shoes of the donor who can help the central character.

3. **Emotional Impact:** How do you want the reader to feel? Angry about the problem? Empathy for the central character? A desire for justice? As you write your story, keep in mind the emotional impact you want the story to have on the reader. The power in the story is getting the reader to feel the emotions in the story. So how do we do that? Tell a story with as much vivid detail as possible so the reader can place themselves into the story.

4. **The Problem:** What is the problem the central character is experiencing that the donor and nonprofit are solving? Describe in detail what the beneficiary's life was like before you got involved, during, and after. Be as descriptive as possible.

5. **The Solution:** What did your organization do to help the central character? How was the donor involved? What is life like now for the beneficiary?

6. **Call to Action:** Now that you've established how the beneficiary was helped, you need to call the reader to action. This may be a donation, or it may be some other call to action such as advocacy or become a volunteer. Connect the reader to what his action will do.

Tell stories of impact to build trust in your potential donor's tribe.

Finally, your nonprofit should be clear with your call to action. When you do participate in a tribe and people become magnetically drawn to your nonprofit, they will want to know how to participate and support the cause.

TOOLS TO ENCOURAGE TRIBAL GIVING

Provide tools to enable supporters to help your organization with little effort or confusion. Lifewater International provides crowdfunding tools to fund clean water in each of the villages it works in with a goal of 1,000 villages completed by 2020. Potential donors are provided an easy-to-use platform to give and to encourage their networks to support the same project. The tools allow tribes to rally around a specific project and see it funded and then track the results as it's completed.

Roxboro Community School, a 10-year-old public charter school in Roxboro, North Carolina, had a major problem: it was ineligible for government funding to assist in bricks and mortar funding needs and needed to create a multipurpose area and gym by renovating a 100-year-old Roxboro Cotton Mill. Instead, the school would need to rely on local fundraising to meet its goals.

The school regularly graduates 100% of its seniors and is consistently ranked in the top 3% of North Carolina public schools. But how does it motivate current and former students and their families, and people in the local community not connected with the school, to contribute to the capital campaign?

The school's board of directors had a vision for a facility that could meet not only the school's needs, but also serve as a venue for the community. The school decided to engage the entire community into the building process and not just stakeholders associated with the school. The school asked community members to join them in the planning process and offer suggestions for the renovation. Their input helped shape the plans for the size and specifications for the renovation so the final building would add much needed event space for the community.

The project was kicked off by a student-run telethon. In just a day and a half, a team of student volunteers raised $100,000 by calling family and local community businesses. Within 12 months, the overall project campaign secured $1.6 million in pledges for the Raise the Roof campaign.

By involving the stakeholders in the planning process and the fundraising campaign, Roxboro Community School created a tribe of people who wanted to see the project come to a successful completion. This initiated the process with $100,000 in fundraising and ultimately resulted in $1.6 million to complete the project.

As you can see from the story of Roxboro Community School, engaging a tribe can help meet the fundraising goal. The school taught us that communication and participation help people feel connected to your cause and more likely to feel a part of your group. As Henri Tafjel taught us, when someone feels a part of your group, she is more likely to be passionately in favor of fellow members of the group.

It isn't your job as a nonprofit marketer to create a brand-new tribe of people who support your organization. Instead, add value to the tribes your donors and potential donors are a part of. You'll find that it is easier and more effective to be a part of a tribe than to create your own.

Marcie Maxwell, Director of National Events & Brand Campaigns, describes relationship building with donors as[18], "The strongest relationships we all have are built on shared experiences. Family bonds are formed over holiday dinners and beach vacations. College memories are born from all-night parties and late-night study sessions. As adults, we forge friendships on work trips and on the Little League sidelines. And as nonprofits, our relationships with our most passionate supporters are no different."

It's not always easy to activate tribes to participate with our nonprofit to fight for a cause. As Pencils of Promise taught us, when you successfully attract people based on their participation in a tribe, you can experience significant financial growth to help more people.

---

[18] https://institute.blackbaud.com/wp-content/uploads/2018/08/Blackbaud_npEXPERTS2018_Final.pdf

TAKE ACTION

1) Write a list of attributes of different donor segments for your nonprofit.

2) Create a list of where your donors congregate. These could be places like:

   a) Social media groups

   b) Conferences

   c) Events

   d) Local meetups

   e) Community activities

The Result: Trustworthiness

Your nonprofit gains the trust of a supporter by demonstrating that the organization accomplishes what it says it will. When the six magnetic attributes align with a donor's heart for giving, you create a donor that trusts your nonprofit.

Lifewater International, a 40-year-old clean water nonprofit, lets donors choose exactly where they want to donate to and then reports back on the progress of the clean water project. For example, I can donate today to Nalongo, Uganda, where 56 families, or 210 people, are waiting for clean water. Lifewater includes a story from a family in the community:

The faces of Tokamuhebwa Habasa and her husband Joram beam with pride at the sight of their children speaking so freely about their hopes and goals.

Justus, age 11, loves English and math, and he wants to become a doctor so he can treat those who are sick and struggle to afford medicine, like his family.

The Habasa family gets their water from a pond they call Nalongo, meaning "mother of twins."

The pond is so vast and deep, its waters never dry up, and seven additional villages travel from afar to gather water from Nalongo.

Although plentiful, the water is badly contaminated.

All eight of the Habasa children attend school currently, but waterborne illnesses threaten them. In recent months, the family visited the health clinic for treatment of typhoid, cholera, and severe diarrhea.

"Every day, a child is sent away from school for delayed payment of school fees and we have to decide between treating those who are sick and returning those who have been sent away from school," Tokamuhebwa said.

Despite their circumstances, the Habasas are positive people, always imagining things will turn out for the best, and placing hope in their children.

"With safe water, the money we currently spend on medication would be invested in keeping them in school," the mother said. "Their studies would not be interrupted, and their chances of success in life would be higher in that case!"

On the project page, Lifewater provides more information to help show you the organization is trustworthy. One section shares the latest project news, while another shows milestones of the progress made. You can explore the community through an interactive map. The fundraiser includes a goal and shows you the donors who recently gave to the project.

All of these points of information help encourage donors to see the organization as trustworthy.

GAIN AND KEEP DONOR TRUST

How to do we gain and keep the trust of potential donors?

First, deliver on your promises. Recent surveys show that one-third of Americans don't trust the charity sector. When a fraudulent organization makes the news, it results in all charities needing to defend their trustworthiness. When you make a promise to your donors, you need to fulfill it. A donor experiences a value exchange when s/he gives. Often, the value received is feeling good. When you make a promise to the donor and break it, the action results in negative emotions that have a stronger impact than the initial "good" feeling the donor experienced. When you break a promise, the net result is a strong negative feeling and potential loss of a donor.

Second, be honest and transparent. As you learned in the Transparency chapter, this magnetic attribute helps a donor feel like s/he *knows* your organization. Make your financials and 990 tax filings readily available. Red Cross is known as one of the most trusted charities. The organization not only posts their annual financial reports but also prepares updates about major disasters responded to a year after the event. These reports include how much money was raised and how it was spent. This kind of transparency builds significant trust with donors.

Third, thank your donors promptly. Whether you send a thank-you video, a note of gratitude, a welcome gift, a thank-you email, or another creative way to thank the donor for their donation, you need to communicate in a specific way to have the biggest impact. Sending your thanks is a key way to continue developing the relationship with your donor. In fact, with 80% of donors stating a thank-you message is the highest motivator for a second gift, properly expressing gratitude is a way to transform your donor file into a healthier one. Timely gratitude communication builds trust with donors.

Fourth, report on the impact of the donation. When a donor makes a gift to your organization, a story loop is opened. The story begins with your donor being a hero to a beneficiary. Explaining what the gift is used for closes the loop with the donor. If you don't close the loop with a donor, s/he will wonder what his/her gift was used for. If you don't share this information, your donor may create assumptions to fill in the gaps you're not filling.

Children International, an international development nonprofit focused on children, shares hundreds of impact stories on their blog at https://www.children.org/stories. These stories often include powerful videos that explain a story in a much more effective way than simply using text.

Fifth, engaging communication involves listening. If you're only talking to donors and not listening to them, you're not communicating. You're simply advertising. Trust requires open communication between your organization and the donor. Open communication is a two-way street, you need to speak to and hear from the donor. When your donor takes an action, thank them. If s/he volunteers, responds to an email, or likes a social media post, acknowledge how much you appreciate his/her support. Create donor surveys where you look for actionable data about what a donor wants — then act when someone responds!

Sixth, building trust requires clarity and consistency. Develop clear messages about what your organization does, who you work with, how you work, and the impact donors have for the cause. When you aren't clear in your messaging or you communicate radically differently with various audiences, you encourage the donor to question the trustworthiness of your organization.

For example, a mid-sized international organization promoted a leader from their programs team into the president role. She began a series of changes in how the organization communicates, focusing on the programmatic model and less on donor-centric communication. The language became more sterile and academic. The appeals became more fact-focused and less story-driven. The communication change caused donors to leave in confusion as they couldn't trust the consistency of the messaging or even comprehend some of it. The organization's revenue dropped 30% in the year after the changes were made. It's vital to maintain trust through clear and consistent messaging.

Seventh, build relationships with your donors. People give when they feel they have a connection with a nonprofit organization. Developing a personal relationship with donors builds trust in your organization.

OneHope, a biblical outreach organization, has a unique model to engage their donors. Instead of employing a team of professional fundraising relationship staff, the organization assigns a group of donors to each employee. From accounting to operations, each OneHope staff member builds a relationship with donors by calling them and asking the donor a simple question, "How can I pray for you?" By building these deep relationships with their Christian donors, OneHope has created a high retention donor program while only spending 4.9% of their revenue on fundraising expenses.

This program also deepens the connection between the employee and OneHope. By encouraging this communication and investment into the lives of donors, OneHope has low staff turnover.

Eighth, set a common goal and vision with your donors. Every good story needs a hero and an enemy. When you set a common goal and vision with your donors, you can do so with a common enemy. For example, your organization may be fighting homelessness. Your audience can share a common vision when they have a shared desire to end homelessness. When you set a vision with your audience to not only fight for somebody or for a cause, but also to fight against a shared enemy, you create trust when you accomplish milestones towards the goal.

At Food for the Hungry, we've had vision, values, and purpose for some time. But, it was difficult for staff to connect with them. A short time ago, we reinvented the vision, values, and purpose into the "FH Heartbeat."

Vision: All forms of human poverty ended worldwide.

Purpose: Together we follow God's call responding to human suffering and graduating communities from extreme poverty.

Values:

- *We follow Jesus*

- *Our work is relational*

- *We invest wisely and focus on results*

- *We serve with humility*

- *We pursue beauty, goodness, and truth*

We have worked hard over the past two years to instill the FH Heartbeat into our staff and our work. We've changed our language to match. We've developed a new strategy with the "Heartbeat" as the foundation. We've seen an increase in employee satisfaction and passion, as we rallied around these core concepts that support and explain why we do the work we do.

Ninth, find ways to create value with members of your audience. One of the fastest ways you can build trust with your audience is to offer something of value that aligns with your cause. For example, if your nonprofit researches autism, offer an eBook on supporting individuals with autism. Autism Speaks provides a number of free resources from special needs financial planning to transitioning to adulthood[19]. These resources create a lot of value for the donor and builds trust that your organization is worthy of support.

Lastly, discover ways to delight your donors. Create "wow" moments that help a donor feel connected to your organization. Surprising donors with demonstrations of gratitude and showing how much they're appreciated helps the donor build a relationship with your organization.

After a donation to a college student support ministry, I received a phone call from the Executive Director thanking me for the gift and asking if there is anything he can do for me. One of the students in the ministry sent me a hand-drawn thank-you card. These two "wow" moments turned me into a lifelong donor.

---

[19] https://www.autismspeaks.org/information-topic

In donor psychology, there is a concept called "reciprocity." When you do something for a donor, s/he feels like s/he needs to reciprocate and perform an action for you. Even small tokens of appreciation can bring goodwill from donors, increasing trust and retention.

Supporters want to know, like, and trust an organization before they commit. With public trust in nonprofit organizations waning, building an organization that is trustworthy will increase connectedness between an organization and its donors, staff, and volunteers.

Nonprofits are among the strongest forces in the world for good. We change lives for millions of people, not only the beneficiaries we serve, but also the people we employ in meaningful work. We help donors feel the joy of giving back. We solve serious problems.

For many of us, knowing the importance of our work keeps us up at night. It can be stressful knowing the impact of our work – and if we miss our strategic plans or fundraising goals, it harms many lives. I've lived through this stress. These magnetic attributes were created to reduce this stress. The Magnetic Nonprofit is one that will continue to grow and transform your beneficiaries' and donors' lives. I'm grateful for the work you're doing, it's so important.

www.ingramcontent.com/pod-product-compliance
Lightning Source LLC
Chambersburg PA
CBHW062057270326
41931CB00013B/3112